Alexandru Calcatinge

Visions of the Real

Stadt- und Raumplanung
Urban and Spatial Planning

Band/Volume 8

LIT

Alexandru Calcatinge

Visions of the Real

An architect's approach
on cultural landscape studies

LIT

For my beloved Family

In memory of Babi

This publication has been funded with support from:
Cover Picture: © by Alexandru Calcatinge

Bibliographic information published by the Deutsche Nationalbibliothek
The Deutsche Nationalbibliothek lists this publication in the Deutsche Nationalbibliografie; detailed bibliographic data are available in the Internet at http://dnb.d-nb.de.

ISBN 978-3-643-90064-7

A catalogue record for this book is available from the British Library

©LIT VERLAG GmbH & Co. KG Wien 2011
Krotenthallergasse 10/8
A-1080 Wien
Tel. +43 (0) 1-409 56 61
Fax +43 (0) 1-409 56 97
e-Mail: wien@lit-verlag.at
http://www.lit-verlag.at

LIT VERLAG Dr. W. Hopf
Berlin 2011
Fresnostr. 2
D-48159 Münster
Tel. +49 (0) 2 51-620 320
Fax +49 (0) 2 51-922 60 99
e-Mail: lit@lit-verlag.de
http://www.lit-verlag.de

Distribution:

In Germany: LIT Verlag Fresnostr. 2, D-48159 Münster
Tel. +49 (0) 2 51-620 32 22, Fax +49 (0) 2 51-922 60 99, e-mail: vertrieb@lit-verlag.de

In Austria: Medienlogistik Pichler-ÖBZ, e-mail: mlo@medien-logistik.at

In Switzerland: B + M Buch- und Medienvertrieb, e-mail: order@buch-medien.ch

In the UK: Global Book Marketing, e-mail: mo@centralbooks.com

In North America by:

Transaction Publishers
New Brunswick (U.S.A.) and London (U.K.)

Transaction Publishers
Rutgers University
35 Berrue Circle
Piscataway, NJ 08854

Phone: +1 (732) 445 - 2280
Fax: + 1 (732) 445 - 3138
for orders (U. S. only):
toll free (888) 999 - 6778
e-mail: orders@transactionpub.com

Table of Contents

Acknowledgements..7
Preface...9

Theoretical approaches..13
Why visions of the real..13
About this book...13
Something about the concepts of vision and real.......................15
Space and time. forms of social sensitivity...................................19
Tracing the concepts at Plato, Aristotle and Kant.......................19
Space and time. Heidegger's meditation......................................27
Language, society and identity. a cultural landscape perspective.....33
Language related to our research. Short introduction................33
Language as a binder..35
Tracing the concept of cultural landscape....................................42
Towards modernity: Modernism and the inter-war architecture.......42
From modernity to the concept of cultural landscape................50
Cultural geography and the birth of a fundamental concept.....53
Architectural and urban visions..72
The cultural landscape as a landscape of power........................82
Psychogeography and the cultural landscape............................85
The flâneur and the observed city..87
Surrealism and the experimental travel.....................................91
The new urbanism and the situationists 96
From daily life to virtual community..105
Virtual space: Heterotopy and tool in the creation and investigation of the cultural landscape..105
A new type of flâneur. The one of virtual space.......................108
The evolution of the studied concept. conclusions...................111

From theory to practice. A comprehensive view.........................115
Case study: cultural planning at a regional level......................115
General presentation of the region...115
Diagnosis..117
Distinctive competences..118
Main disfunctionalities and their effects.................................120
Possible development strategy...121

- Implementation..122
- A model for the region..124
- Vision, mission and guiding principles..124
- Conclusions of the case study...126
- Workshop essay. A good practice example..129
  - Remixing Architecture..129
  - Presenting the theme..129
  - Organizing the workshop..131
  - The project of studio 6...135
  - It is possible!..138
- The future of Symbolic Places..140
  - People objects – Studio 9...140
- Bibliography..141
- Illustration Index...148
- Alphabetical Index..149
- About the Author...152

Acknowledgements

First and foremost I would like to thank HR Prof. h. c. Univ.-Doz. Dr. Peter Jordan, from the Austrian Academy of Sciences in Vienna, for his valuable guidance and advice, who appreciated my work and without whom this book wouldn't have been possible, and also for his PhD advisory in Vienna.

Secondly, I would like to convey thanks to Dr. Arthur Spiegler and Dr. Brigitte Macaria, from ECOVAST Austria, for sharing valuable information and invaluable assistance in this project and in many others during my stay in Vienna.

I would also like to express my deepest gratitude to my PhD supervisor from Romania, Prof. Dr. Arh. Alexandru Sandu, dean of the Urban Planning Faculty from the University of Architecture and Urban Planning „Ion Mincu" in Bucharest for his valuable guidance through research on this great subject; to Prof. Dr. Arh. Hanna Derer, head of the Doctoral School SD-SITT, for her invaluable assistance, support and guidance; to Prof. Dr. Helmut Wohlschlaegl, head of the Department of Geography and Regional Research from the University of Vienna, for his acceptance to continue my PhD research at his department for a full academic year.

Special thanks goes to Carabas Ioan Constantin, for his help with the creation of this book's official website, and also to Carabas Nicoleta who did great work by translating most the contents of this book. Her help was invaluable and couldn't have done it in such a short time without her.

I wish to express my love and gratitude to my beloved family, for their understanding and endless support through the duration of this project, especially to my dearest sister, Mirona, and my beloved parents, whose help was of great value in writing this book. I would also like to thank all my friends who supported me during all this time, therefore my deepest gratitude and love goes to Amelia, for her acceptance to publish images of her paintings in this book.

Special thanks also goes to Richard Kisling, from Lit Verlag, who was of great help in guiding me to finish the book, and to Marcel Piteiu, general manager of Romgaz S.A for the financial support for publishing this book.

Preface

In our world of highly specialized, fragmented knowledge, synoptic, holistic works have become rare exceptions. This book is an example of this rare species. It is fascinating, how an architect – usually destined to exert the wishes of clients and to draft buildings according to functional, admittedly also aesthetic requirements – considers the whole context, the preconditions as well as the consequences of his actions. However, he is not "only" an architect, but also a spatial planner. And this explains already a lot.

In the manner of philosophical circles he proceeds from the general to the specific starting with the concept(s) of time and (geographical) space referring to Aristotle, Kant, Heidegger and others. Culture and landscape and their mutual relation are the next topic; the relative meanings of space and place is another one. He discusses the role of language and place names for space-related identity building and ends up with the urban landscape or cityscape as a representation of culture, social conditions and power, as a complex of symbols and signs that has to be interpreted: "The urban cultural landscape is like a theatrical stage, a frame full of symbols in which the parade of power take place, a power represented in most cases by the political" (p. 82). Having followed this impressive spiral from space to the city, a case study of cultural planning in the Transilvanian region of Târnava Mare and the report of a workshop on urban planning in the Socialist-type Bratislavian suburb Petržalka appear to the reader just as appendices. The term "cultural planning" is in this context applied at least not far from what is otherwise understood by "endogenous development".

It is obvious that such a wide *tour d'horizon* within the small size of a booklet cannot cover all features extensively, and it is inevitable that sometimes questions are rather raised than answered. But this will prompt further discussion and has its merits in this way.

One focal point in this respect is the relation between space and place and how the "feeling of place" in the sense of Yi-Fu Tuan can be promoted. This is, of course, a crucial question for an architect, when he conceives himself not just as a technician, but as engaged in shaping an appropriate environment for a community of human beings. And it is legitimate and understandable when he arrives at the opinion that people develop a sense of place, an emotional attachment to place not only as a function of time, but also due to "unusual composition of space and form" (Illustration 1 on p. 65). If this was so, the architect – and also the spatial planner – had indeed a paramount function in space-related identity building. But I am not sure, whether this is so. Maybe I am inclined to take emotional roots extremely easily; but it happens to me that I feel attached to a very normal hotel room already after some days and feel a kind of sadness, when I have finally to depart. This happens perhaps, since time is not just an empty vessel, but occasionally full of events, of actual and mental experiences – especially when you are not at home, but on vacations or attending conferences. And all these experiences get connected and linked with the place from where you depart in the morning and to where you return in the evening. Even if this place is actually nothing than the place to rest and sleep. If this was not so, why then would people inhabiting an unspectacular landscape get very often not less attached to their "place" than permanent dwellers of high-ranking and exceptional tourist attractions? Emotional attachment to a place is certainly not just a function of landscape spectacularity and due to an unusual composition of space and form.

Another interesting point for further discussion is the spatial range of "place" in the sense of this section of space to which a certain community feels to be emotionally attached. This question has – so the reader is learning from this book – already been raised by Aristotle in "Politics", but it is far from being resolved and still answered differently up to our days. This question refers especially to larger geographical features such as mountain ranges, plains, streams and seas, which do not end at the horizon.

Up to which distance develop local communities emotional ties in these cases? Are these ties – for instance in the case of seas – confined to coastal waters, where people are used to go for a swim and where they are cruising with their vessels and fisher boats? Or are they also extended to the high sea, even to parts of it far beyond the horizon? Do people inhabiting one end of a mountain range like the Alps or the Carpathians feel emotionally attached to all its parts, even to very remote places at the other end? Does a Viennese recognize the Danube near Giurgiu in Romania, i.e. at its lower run and approximately 1,000 km from his/her home, as the same river and the same water that has (much) earlier passed his own city? Will he/she have a more intimate feeling, when watching these waters flow, will he/she even claim to be emotionally as close to them as the local population?

More generally speaking: Is a geographical feature always subject to the feel of place in its entirety? Is the mental construct of a geographical feature so powerful that it can influence emotions to such an extent?

And how is it with the feel for countries? Obviously, many citizens of a country feel to be attached to the whole country as a spatial construct. But occurs this attachment really at the same level as the attachment to meadows, woods and hills surrounding one's house and village? Isn't it rather of a symbolic and therefore quite different kind?

The author of this book goes even as far as to highlight the role of place names in space-related identity building, their role in turning "space" into "place". This seems to be a far-fetched topic, but it is not, since place names have indeed two functions in this respect: the function both of labels and of supporting emotional ties.

In the symbolic function of a label a place name represents a space-related concept filled with contents. The name conveys these contents to inhabitants of the place as well as to people from the outside insofar the latter know these contents or have learned about them (as this is, e.g., the case with tourism marketing). In this function place names are very similar to flags or coats of arms. It is characteristic for strong space-related identities that their names are reflected many times, e.g. in names of restaurants, hotels, dishes, ships, trains, newspapers etc. How burdened with emotions the label function of place names is can be derived from two facts: (1) administrations often refuse linguistic minorities the official use of their place names and interpret this use as a territorial claim; (2) in multilingual areas official use of minority place names frequently stirs up conflict among the local population. Naming is conceived as having the power of defining the identity of a place.

The function of supporting emotional ties affects only persons well-acquainted with a certain place, e.g. a cultural landscape. These are in the first line inhabitants; secondly also people, who have been socialised in a certain place and later left it; thirdly also persons, who have only in a later stage of their life found a certain emotional relation to a place, e.g. as frequent vacationers. For them mentioning or memorising a name means to strengthen "the feel of a place" according to Yi-Fu Tuan and to let the emotional tie with it grow. In this function place names are an important factor of "feeling at home".

So it can indeed be said that the naming of landscapes and places in general is an essential contribution to space-related identity building, to the building of personal as well as of group identities. This is all the more important in a globalising and secularising world, when other identifiers are losing ground.

It is perhaps not really a surprise that such a profound and sensitive encounter of the cultural landscape has been written by a colleague from Romania. Like most of the post-Socialist countries Romania displays an impressive impact of blunt Socialist architecture and landscape transformation, of which especially suburbs and the capital Bucharest with its bombastic House of People are striking examples. But perhaps more than some other post-Socialist countries Romania disposes also over a variety of traditional cultural landscapes. And the author, socialised in one of them and well-acquainted with most of them, may by this contrast well have been hinted at the mechanisms of and the powers behind the shaping of cultural landscapes.

I'm sure that this book will stimulate the discussion on space-related identity building and the role of architects and spatial planners in it decisively.

HR Prof. h. c. Univ.-Doz. Dr. Peter Jordan, Vienna.

THEORETICAL APPROACHES

WHY VISIONS OF THE REAL

ABOUT THIS BOOK

The idea for this book came in 2009, when I was preparing a paper for an international conference that was held in Austria the following year. The paper from that conference was published later in the *International Journal of Arts and Sciences* in 2010, Volume 3, Number 8 in the United States of America, and was the core for this book. Thus came the idea to publish a book on cultural landscape studies.

Therefore, this book brings together the most important and relevant ideas for my PhD research, and have been brought to a form that would permit the reader to follow the most important arguments that this book brings. You will find writings on different topics, all related in my personal opinion, to the cultural landscape studies.

After a short introduction to the concepts of vision and real, the reader will then discover the interesting aspects of time and space in the study of cultural landscapes, the role of language in cultural identity formation, and after that, the attention will be on the roots of cultural landscape concept and its transformations in architecture and geography, with regard to the evolution of cultural geography and psycho geography, and the virtual existence of the contemporary individual. The last part of the book will create the bridge from theory to practice at a regional level, with regard to the cultural planning process as a tool for regional development, by presenting a paper that was first created for the master's degree, and after that presented at the *3rd Conference of the Adriatic Forum* in September 2010 in Vienna. After that, two essays will be presented in the last part, regarding two workshops on urban planning, as examples of good practice.

Thus, being an architect involves understanding concepts that we have to work with but we have to take into consideration different approaches from different fields of study. As being involved in the creative process, architects should understand what surrounds them and to give a special meaning to their creation. Thus, the second meaning of vision, as regards the foreseeing, is closely related to the process of creation in which the architect is the most important actor.

The cultural landscape is what lies around us, more or less, it is what has to be understood and learned to deal with. All this in order to create for the future and for a better community. This doesn't mean that we will try to explain everything about the cultural landscape. It is impossible. What we will try to do is to present what we believe to be the most important concepts and theories of the most prominent people that studied the concept and from the ones that somehow invented it. And the best way to do this is to start from the beginning in order to understand the contemporary iterations of the concept. We will not reinvent the concept, but we will try to understand it by presenting the concept in the view of most important thinkers of the twentieth century.

It is a hard task, but this we believe to be only the foundation for future studies in cultural landscapes. For this, we have studied different concepts from philosophy, geography, language studies, architecture and urban planning in order to give a short sketch for a more comprehensive study on cultural landscapes.

Why visions of the real and what is the relation with the cultural landscape? How does these two phrases connect to each other? We like to consider the cultural landscape as part of a reality that is seen and visioned different by each individual. This means that the concept has an almost infinite number of meanings and ways to see and understand it. This book presents some of the visions of the surrounding reality, as the most known ones and most important in the evolution of cultural studies and landscapes.

SOMETHING ABOUT THE CONCEPTS OF VISION AND REAL

The sensitivity of space is given to us by the senses with which we perceive it, by the way we perceive its configuration and the way in which we carry it out. The tactile space is fragmented, with no possibility of delimitation, being on an unlimited field. The visual space is a limited space, being limited by the horizon and which can be caught with the eye. The visual space is a plural space[1]. There are different interpretations of the two senses. Through tactile, touching we go towards things, we create space through our proximity, by exploration and sensorial sensitivity. Through sight we bring things to us, what seemed unlimited now can be seen, can be brought close or can produce certain sensitivity by overwhelming. Through their complementarity the two senses lead us to liberation and achievement at the same time.

The word vision is a very complex one. It incorporates the act of seeing the outside world, and in another sense it has a more abstract understanding as it also means a way of imagination, a way of seeing things, a way to project images.[2] Vision, through imagination and creative process, has the power to transcend space and time and gives the human the ability to create mental images, as we will see further in this book as regards the city as a mental construct.[3]

As it is well known, we live in a world in which the sense of vision is the dominating one over the others and architecture is what helps us to relate to reality, in space and time, and

> it domesticates limitless space and endless time to be tolerated, inhabited and understood by humankind.[4]

---

[1] Troscianko 2010, p. 152. Emily Troscianko wrote: "The continuity of visual experience which we may conceive of as a Jamesian flowing stream has often been characterized as a sequence of images succeeding one another in a sort of internal picture show, or inner theater. (...) seeing requires that we build up a detailed picture of a situation as we enter it: we make rapid eye movements, or saccades, around the scene, and take in visual information through the eyes, which is transmitted to the brain, where the information is processed to create a mental, picture-like representation of the scene".

[2] Cosgrove 2008, p. 5. Denis Cosgrove wrote in the introduction of his book: "Vision in the sense of active seeing is inescapable in the practice of geography. (...) Geographical description, which performs the task of interrogating, synthesizing and representing the diversity of environments, places and people, has traditionally sought to present its audience with rich and compelling visual images".

[3] Cosgrove 2008, p. 8 : "Vision's meaning incorporates imagination: the ability to create images in the mind's eye, which exceed in various ways those registered on the retina of the physical eye by light from the external world. Vision has a creative capacity that can transcend both space and time: it can denote foreseeing as well as seeing".

[4] Pallasmaa 2005, p. 17.

It is an era of production images[5], when our reality is clearly build upon a structure of media production symbols, and the city is like a collage of different mental images that are arranged in a specific way to form the architectural reality in a world that is ruled by time and speed. Juhani Pallasmaa argues that

> one of the reasons why the architectural and urban settings of our time tend to make us feel like outsiders (…) is their poverty in the field of peripheral vision[6]

and that

> the hegemony of vision has been reinforced in our time by a multitude of technological inventions and the endless multiplication and production of images.[7]

In order to continue our argument, lets remember Frampton's critical regionalism which he described as it

> emphasizes the tactile as much as the visual.[8]

With regard to philosophy, the discourse of vision has its own history, and even more than that, as Veronique Foti argued,

> it also has traced (…) the delicate border that separates and conjoins the visible and the invisible.[9]

Regarding our cultural landscape studies, what we find here as a reference to the invisible is closely related to the imaginative and in some cases virtual side that the cultural landscapes implies.

As strange as it may seam, some architects were (and still are) influenced by Martin Heidegger's writings, being frequently cited in their theoretical approaches. As there is a full sub chapter dedicated to Heidegger's concepts of

---

[5] Stout 2000, p. 146. Quote: „If the architecture of the city could present images of foreboding power or lyrical freedom, it was nonetheless the lives of the people of the city themselves that became the constantly recurring theme of photo-journalists and artists alike. (…) The project of comprehending the modern city visually played, and continues to play, a central role in the history of art and consciousness. The great themes of the city – its kinetic activity, its juxtapositions and ironies, its massive forms and tiny details – provided the artist with a subject matter that could not be ignored and pioneered modes of visual perception and communication that were to fundamentally transform the nature of social life. (…) Eventually, the new modes of visual perception would be connected to narrative – particularly to the <<urban narratives>> of young rural innocents encountering the experience of the city for the first time (…). And out of the interconnection of urban narrative and visual representation would come cinema, the ultimate realization of the kinetic imagery that urban life characterized and photography mirrored".
[6] Pallasmaa 2005, p. 13.
[7] Pallasmaa 2005, p. 21.
[8] Frampton 2007, p. 327.
[9] Foti 2003, p. 2.

time and space, regarding vision we will make a short reference to Veronique Foti, as we find her writings on the matter of visions, visuality and invisible as most important, in order to follow our argument on our visions of the real.[10]

Even though it was an essay on technology[11] and the transformations of the modern world, his ideas we consider to be really important for our studies:

> One of the essential phenomena of the modern age is its science. (…) A third equally essential phenomenon of the modern period lies in the event of art's moving into the purview of aesthetics. That means that the art work becomes the object of mere subjective experience, and that consequently art is considered to be an expression of human life. A fourth modern phenomenon manifests itself in the fact that human activity is conceived and consummated as culture. Thus culture is the realization of the highest values, through the nurture and cultivation of the highest goods of man. It lies in the essence of culture, as such nurturing, to nurture itself in its turn and thus to become the politics of culture.[12]

As we can find out from the upper quote, in Heidegger's essay is very clear stated the fact that culture gained a new role, being part of a modern phenomenon, thus it became part of the social experience of the individuals at a clear subjective level.

Thus, the social experience is only a part of much bigger system, as Merleau-Ponty argued:

> The hole system of experience – world, own body and empirical self – are subordinated to a universal thinker charged with sustaining the relationships between the three terms.[13]

And this kind of experience, as any kind of experience, is governed by perception, which links the body with the outside world. So, the experience of the individual with the outside world is done in two distinct ways: bodily or

---

[10] Foti 2003, pp. 81-82. Veronique Foti starts chapter six with regard to Heidegger's work called *The Time of the World Picture* and she argued that: "the world picture, as he understands it, is not a spontaneous, or culturally specific, symbolic image that one might form of the world (such as, for instance, a mandala) but rather the sort of picture that allows one to <<get the picture>> (*im Bilde zu sein*) and to use it for the purpose of installing oneself in the world understood as the totality of beings. The picture at stake here is not visual in any significant sense; rather, what visuality it may possess is schematic or diagrammatic and serves to facilitate human self-orientation, with a view to technological, or technologically inspired, productivity and mastery. It functions as the quasi-visual encoding of the parameters of a legitimating projective conception that is, as such, of the order of the invisible. The loss of visuality involved is not merely a loss of seeing but also a loss of being looked at and seen".

[11] Arthur Kroker, in an online article published in 2002 entitled Hyper-Heidegger, described Heidegger as „the theorist par excellence of the digital future". Website: http://www.ctheory.net/articles.aspx?id=348 accesed on 10th of october 2010 at 23.07.

[12] Heidegger 1977, p. 116.

[13] Merleau-Ponty 2009, p. 241.

mentally, thus the cultural landscape becomes an embodiment of a concept where imagination and vision are associated with the real. Is a reality that is produced by a hybrid cultural space. The space we are talking about is a space of social interaction and where, as Heidegger said, human activity is consummated as culture. Is this the space of reality? Beatriz Jaguaribe said:

> Similarly to the temporal instant that is lived and yet cannot be consciously understood until it has been processed by memory and language, the real is a disputed category that tests the limits of representation and exceeds the selective mechanisms of our conscious control. As a presence of the world beyond and outside our selves, the real cannot be fully encompassed by our experience, and even experience itself becomes elusive while we are in the process of living it. By contrast, as has often been remarked, reality is a part of the real that has been processed by the cultural construction of society.[14]

Furthermore, the author uses the term *shock of the real*[15] with regard to the postmodern media productions in the urban spaces. Is probably what Heidegger prefigured at the beginning of the century, that the existance has a cultural side, and what Debord described in the 60's as the society of spectacle, and later on, the cultural moment and the new economy and globalization[16] gave us the real shock of the contemporary urban existence.

Therefore, as a conclusion, we may ask if the cultural landscape, as a concept, is somehow a vision of the real. By making this short presentation of the two terms, we could argue that reality, as our perception of the outside world through the filter of our mind, is part of the spatial perception that we have on what surrounds us. Thus, every one of us has a vision of the real that is the cultured landscape around us, and the way we see it is transfigured in the way we act and the way we relate to our surroundings. Our relations with other individuals, our involvement in the community, and our lives in the urban spaces are all related to our perception of space[17].

---

[14] Jaguaribe 2005, p. 69.
[15] Jaguaribe 2005, p. 70. Beatriz Jaguaribe wrote:"By the term *shock of the real*, I am referring to specific representations in both written narrative and visual imagery that unleash an intense, dramatic discharge that destabilizes notions of reality itself. The <<shock>> element resides in the nature of the event that is portrayed and in the convincing usage that emphasizes a <<reality effect>> that nevertheless disrupts normative patterns".
[16] Inglis 2010, p. 136. David Inglis wrote:"The forces of globalization are also seen to create new forms of trans-national territories, spaces and terrains, both material and at the level of cultural imaginaries. While different theorists of globalization may disagree on when, to put it crudely, globalization processes <<started>>, there is broad agreement that the period since 1945 has witnessed the most intense and far-reaching phase of globalizing tendencies, with the effect that the last 60 years or so of world history seem particularly qualitatively unlike previous epochs.

Space and time. Forms of social sensitivity

Tracing the concepts at Plato, Aristotle and Kant

Since Antiquity the understanding of the concepts space and time was a fundamental thing for answering to certain questions regarding the being. Parmenides and Heraclites regarded the being from the perspective of continuity, of passing of time and of a sequentiality. Chronos as a human relation with space and time, was resembled with the flow of a river, or the passing of time was seen as an arrow from past to future. Thus, the physical qualities of time and space got to be differentiated by a distinct form of time from now, of the moment and the space understood as kairos.

With Plato and Aristotle this problem gets to be divided. The being becomes some kind of a spiritual problem and space a physical dimension. Then in the next centuries space and time will become physical categories without any relation to the individual, becoming absolute time and absolute space, or they will be considered experimental artifices created by man. For example, determining time at Aristotle as a series of moments will determine later on time to be perceived as a physical quantifying concept, and then Newton and Descartes as well as the British empirics will perceive space and time as things which request less effort from people and later Nietzsche interpreted time as nothing else but a tool of man. Closer to our times, in the 20th century time and space were perceived as quantifying elements of nature.

The world, the material and time are introduced in the class of metaphysical concepts. The concepts can be introduced in two relatively distinct classes, the class of objective metaphysical concepts, mental elaborations which reflect a self and the class of subjective metaphysical concepts, where

---

[17] Merleau-Ponty 2009, p. 327. Maurice Merleau-Ponty wrote: "The traditional problem of the perception of space and perception generally must be reintegrated into a vaster problem. (...) each express perception occurring in my journey through Paris – the cafes, people's faces, the poplars along the quays, the bends of the Seine – stands out against the city's whole being, and merely confirms that there is a certain style or a certain significance which Paris possesses. (...) There is present a latent significance, diffused throughout the landscape or the city, which we find in something specific and self-evident which we fell no need to define. (...) Every perception presupposes, on the perceiving subject's part, a certain past, and the abstract function of perception, as a coming together of objects, implies some more occult act by which we elaborate our environment".

mental elaborations belong, which are considered as not having any direct relation with an external being.

The time, which Plato suggests is a time somehow exterior to the human being, such as the cosmic time, which coincides with the circle movement of days and nights, months and years. The fundamental property of this time is reversibility. The periodic time he conceives, that time of cyclic reversibility is nothing else than the ideatic reflex of a pure experience and the name conferred to the initial confess of senses[18]. But Plato sustains on the other hand that time is also a copy or a mobile image of eternity[19].

And in the conception of Aristotle the existence of a soulless time is accepted (meaning with no thinking soul), of an exterior time identified with the succession of processes and phenomena, which characterize things and which is made perceptible only through senses[20]. He says that no authentic reflection related to time is possible without the introduction in the equation of soul as indispensable reference element. First we should take into consideration the pure life of the soul, its movement from anterior to posterior. To this rather mystic experience an experience is added which is based on the experience of the senses which determine us to settle an order of succession in the development of phenomena and events as well as a periodicity in this order. By the introversion of such a form of existence and its subjection to the sense capacity we get to the definition of time as a number (that is the magnitude or the magnitude of the movement after the anterior and posterior).

The essence of time is no longer present in the exterior of soul but is transformed in its interior, reduced to the statute of a numerical concept. But Aristotle does not stop here; he moves the initial accent on the sky idea to the moment idea. This does not mean that Aristotle will define time as the unit of the movement number after anterior and posterior, but he will be satisfied with making of the moment something without which time could simply not be understood. In its quality as unit of a number which measures, delimitative of the anterior and posterior, the moment is permanently one and the same, identical with itself, which is outside time belonging to eternity. The moment lends to the number whose constituent is the character of eternal identity. It instruments, thus, the reception of time as a paradox eternal time, in other words a metaphysical time.

---

[18] Plato 2008, p. 26 (38a-b).
[19] Plato 2008, p. 25(37d).
[20] Aristotle 2008, p. 115 (223a).

If we try to identify the main ideas of a philosophy on time we have to speak about several coordinates. On the one hand the idea that time represents the continuation of a series of processes and phenomena specific to the individual beings and ensembles, which they comprise, and on the other hand the affirmation of the idea that there is a reversible time and an irreversible time. The reversible time could be defined as a property of the configurations and systems of the physical universe, although not all processes of the universe have such a character, because there are processes and phenomena, which distinguish by their irreversible nature. The structures and systems of the physical and biological world are characterized both by reversibility and irreversibility. But it should be mentioned that irreversibility will achieve a profounder level of the being within the living individuals than of objects specific to the physical universe. On the other hand reversibility implies a passing from one state to another, a movement, a development, the moments through which reversibility passes do only rediscover already known states and phenomena.

In his *Physics,* Aristotle had a profound discussion about the nature, about what we call now natural science. We could extrapolate this to what could be the very early beginning of understanding the nature of natural and what now we call cultural as regarding the landscape and the human intervention. By that time, all the technologies that are present in our lifes now didn't exist. That is why his argument has a different understanding nowadays. In his study of nature, Aristotle had some interesting points to discuss. Some of them, as the one cited in in the next paragraph, are very important in our acceptance for the understanding and evolution of the concept of cultural landscape:

> Some things exist by nature, others are due to other causes. Natural objects include animals and their parts, plants and simple bodies like earth, fire, air, and water; at any rate, we do say that these kinds of things exist naturally. The obvious difference between all this things and things which are not natural is that each of the natural ones contains within itself a source of change and of stability, in respect of eighter movement or increase and decrease or alteration.[21]

This is how the philosopher started his chapter on the nature of things, argueing that every natural thing has a nature. Furthermore, he asks if the nature of the thing is its matter or its form.

> Some people take the nature and substance of any natural thing to be its primary component, something which is unformed in itself. (…) An alternative

---

[21] Aristotle 2008, p. 33 (192b8).

is to think of it as the shape and form which enables us to define what an object is.[22]

For Aristotle, place and space can not be conceived without a reporting to sensitive means. The sensitive body and its movement are unconceivable without reporting to a special place.[23] This movement coincides with drifting, locomotion. But according to Aristotle there are two types of locomotion, a linear movement and a cyclic movement[24]. The linear movement characterizes the movement of the bodies to become, to generate and to destroy (the four primordial sublunary elements and the things that are based on these elements), and the circular movement characterizes the incorruptible bodies uncreated and eternal, that is the actual celestial bodies. The linear movement has a beginning and an end; it is temporally finite, meaning it is imperfect, while the circular movement has no beginning and no end, that becomes continuous and infinite[25]. Aristotle defines place as a space limited by the margins of the containing body. We could compare the place with the medium of any pot, which includes both the extremities of the pot and its inner part. We could say that the place is from this perspective the immediate unmoveable limit of the thing which contains the very condition of conceiving that limit not only as a simple not modifiable exteriority of the containing body.[26]

---

[22] Aristotle 2008, p. 35 (193a9-a30).
[23] Aristotle 2008, pp. 78-79 (208b1-b27). In *Phisics, book IV*, Aristotle tries to answer a difficult question regarding the existance of place. „The phenomenon of replacement seems to make it clear that there is such a thing as place. (…) Secondly, the movements of the simple natural bodies show not only that there is such a thing as place, but also that it has a certain power. (…) thirdly, those who claim that void exists are really talking about place, since what they mean by <<void>> is probably place deprived by body. These facts support the idea that there is such a thing as place, in addition to body, and that every perceptible body is in place. (…) In other words, he shares the common belief that everything is somewhere – that is, in some place. And if place is like that, then it would be truly remarkable and prior to everything, since that which is a prerequisite for other things to exist, but whose existence does not depend on other things, is bound to be primary. The point here is that place is not distroyed when the things it contains are destroyed".
[24] Aristotle 2008, pp. 211-227 (259b32-266a6).
[25] Aristotle 2008, p.214 (261a23). Aristotle says: „The most important point, however, is that this kind of change – change of place – is clearly the kind which, strictly speaking, a self-changer causes. But in our view it is a self-changer which is, out of all the things which are changed and which cause change, the original source and the primary cause of the change of changing things".
[26] Aristotle 2008, pp. xx-xxi. David Bostock, wrote in the introduction of Aristotle's *Physics*: „It opens with the thought that a natural object, as opposed to one made by man, has within itself its own source of change. (…) For it seems equally true that a natural object – an animal, a plant, an element such as earth – does not have in itself the source of *its own* production. (…) is there really, in principle, any distinction between natural objects and others?".

In *Politics,* Aristotle also talks about limits when he asks a legitimate question about the city:

> When are men, living in the same place, to be regarded as a single city – what is the limit? Certainly not the wall of the city, for you might surround Peloponnesus with a wall. Like this, we may say, is Babylon, and every city that has the compass of a nation rather than a city.[27]

He argues how the city can be defined by its proper function and by its citizens, as they all form an nucleus who's aim is the good of everyone. Even though, he sees the city at the same time as a hole and a group of independent parts, especially in *Politics I* where the family is the central theme, as the primary association for the necessities of life. Thus, he was the one that raised the problem of studying the city, even though it appeared to be impossible by that time. The city was a apparently enormous group of different parts, and in the first book of *Politics* the parts were divided at the smallest level – the household, which by itself was a nucleus that had several smaller parts (the family members and the slaves) that themselves were part of the larger nucleus that was the entire city. Thus he talks about the evolution of the citizen and the community, starting from the family, the house, the village and the city:

> the partnership therefore that comes about in the course of nature for everyday purposes is the 'house' (…) on the other hand the primary partnership made up of several households for the satisfaction of not mere daily needs is the village. (…)The partnership finally composed of several villages is the city-state; it has at last attained the limit of the virtually complete self-sufficiency, and thus, while it comes into existence for the sake of life, it exists for the good life.[28]

Aristotle considered that space has in itself several dimensions: length, breadth, depth, those being dimensions of the bodies being equivalent with the natural directions towards which the bodies move.

Later, during the Enlightenment, another known conception about time and space belongs to Immanuel Kant, who broadly develops this issue in *The Critique of Pure Reason* but also in *Prolegomena to Any Future Metaphysics*. Immanuel Kant was the central figure of modern philosophy and sought to rebuild philosophy from the ground up, by permanently changing its problems and methods. In his most known and important work[29], *The Critique of*

---

[27] Aristotle 2008, p. 34.
[28] Aristotle 1959, pp. 7-9 (1252b).
[29] Adorno 2001, p. 4. Theodor W. Adorno, in one of his lectures from 12ᵗʰ of may 1959 stated the following regarding the work of Kant: „I cannot deny that I still believe that this work is one that deserves the very greatest respect. It does so for quite objective reasons, albeit for

Pure Reason[30], Kant is isolating a priori elements in the Aesthetic, like time and space, and he classifies those concepts, by giving both methaphysical and transcendental expositions.[31] An extensive explanation of both expositions is given by Graham Bird in his book *The Revolutionary Kant*. Explaining the methaphysical expositions, Graham Bird firstly explains the use of the term a priori[32] and the use of new words in Kant's vocabulary:

> In the first metaphysical exposition Kant provides an immediate statement of his position: Space is a form of outer sense and time a form of inner sense.[33]

Bird also makes a short classification of Kant's metaphysical expositions, in which space and time are regarded as a priori and intuitive:

> (1) Space and time are already presupposed in empirical representations of their relations. (2) The absence of space and time cannot be represented, but we can represent them as empty of objects (appearance). (...) (4) Neither space nor time is discursive or general; they signify only one space or one time and so are

---

reasons that are very different from those to which it owed its position when it first appeared. What I should like is to make this book speak to us."

[30] Kant 2000, p. 157 (B37-B38). Kant wrote: „By means of outer sense (a property of our mind) we represent to ourselves objescts as outside us, and all as in space. In space their form, magnitude, and relation to one another is determined, or determinable. Inner sense, by means of which the mind intuits itself, as an object, yet it is still a determinate form, under which the intuition of its inner determinations is represented in relations of time. Time can no more be intuited externally than space can be intuited as something in us".

[31] Kant 2000, p. 155 (B34-A20). Kant wrote: „In whatever way and through whatever means a cognition may relate to objects, that through which it relates immediately to them, and at which all thought as a means is directed as an end, is intuition. (...) The capacity (receptivity) to acquire representations through the way in which we are affected by objects is called sensitivity. Objects are therefore given to us by means of sensibility, ant it alone affords us intuitions; but they are thought through the understanding, and from it arise concepts. (...) The effect of an object on the capacity for representation, insofar as we are affected by it, is sensation. That intuition which is related to the object through sensation is called empirical. The undetermined object of an empirical intuition is called appearance. I call that in the appearance which corresponds to sensation its matter, but that which allows the manifold of appearance to be intuited as ordered in certain relations I call the form of appearance. Since that within which the sensations can alone be ordered and placed in a certain form cannot itself be in turn sensation, the matter of all appearance is only given to us *a posteriori*, but its form must all lie ready for it in the mind *a priori,* and can therefore be considered separately from all sensation."

[32] Bird 2006, pp. 89-90. Graham Bird used two graphical schemes to present the use of transcendent and transcendental in Kant's works and the use of the words a priori and a posteriori.

[33] Bird 2006, p. 106. Graham Bird wrote: „the metaphysical expositions are so called because they are designed to represent <<clearly, though not necessarily exhaustively>> what a concept such as space or time contains <<as given a priori>>. Kant's references to <<concepts>> of space and time and to what is <<given a priori>> underline important points. (...) The outcome of the strategy, that space and time are a priori forms of sense, is represented by saying that space and time are both a priori intuitions.

intuitive. Apodeictically certain principles of space and time cannot be derived solely from concepts, and require a priori intuitions. (5) Space and time are represented as infinite or unlimited. Their parts are determined only through limitation and this distinguishes them from general concepts.[34]

Furthermore, Kant's transcendental expositions are about accepting synthetic a priori knowledge. Thus, Bird argued that:

> The arguments claim that only space's a priori intuitive character could make intelligible the possibility of geometry as a body of synthetic a priori knowledge; and that only time's similar character could make possible synthetic a priori knowledge of motion.[35]

An explanation on the term a priori judgements is given also by Adorno, and we find it much more easy to understand:

> What I now owe you is an explanation of the enormous importance ascribed to these synthetic *a priori* judgements, however they are to be understood in detail. We are talking here of judgements which are valid independently of experience or which hold good for all future experience. (…) We are generally interested – at a fairly basic level – to know whether these judgements suffice for us to orientate ourselves and, after that, whether they possess enough plausability, power and penetration, or however you want to phrase it.[36]

Kant develops his conception about time introducing as absolute reference term the inner constitution of the subject. But for him time is no inherent determination of the phenomena of the spiritual life, but a transcendental condition of their development. He talks about the transcendental doctrine of elements[37] which in the first part is represented by the transcendental aesthetic, where questions are raised on the subject of time and space.

Time is a pure form, a formal frame necessary for all determined inner institutions, a primordial representation about myself[38], as a content empty subjective duration, a representation, which makes possible all the other representations (content full) about my inner life. This a priori representation is an intuition not a concept:

---

[34] Bird 2006, p. 107.
[35] Bird 2006, p. 108.
[36] Adorno 2001, p. 23.
[37] Kant 2000, p. 156 (A21-B36). Kant wrote: „I call a science af all principles of *a priori* sensibility the transcendental aesthetic. There must therefore be such a science, which constitutes the first part of the transcendental doctrine of elements, in contrast to that which contains the principles of pure thinking, and is named transcendental logic".
[38] Kant 2000, p. 163 (B50). Kant wrote: „time is nothing other the form of inner sense, ot the intuition of our self and our inner state".

> Time is not an empirical concept that is somehow drawn from an experience. For simultaneity or succession would not themselves come into perception if the representation of time did not ground them *a priori*. Only under its presupposition can one represent that several things exist at one and the same time (simultaneously) or in different times (successively).[39]

That is not an empiric concept, because representation of time is not taken out from any sensitive experience. Thus, simultaneity and succession, the only representations which could lead to an empiric data bases, do not become perception elements only if the representation of time serves them a priori, as a fundament, we could say. But the representation of time as a unique duration prior to perception and simultaneity or the succession in which the inner phenomena are integrated. Thus, we first have the representation of a unique time, of an intuition and only then we can form the concept of different times, deducing them form this intuition:

> Our assertions accordingly teach the empirical reality of time, (i.e., objective validity) in regard to all objects that may ever be given to our senses. And since our intuition is always sensible, no object can ever be given to us in experience that would not belong under the condition of time. But, on the contrary, we dispute all claim of time to absolute reality, namely where it would attach to things absolutely as a condition or property even without the senses. In this therefore consists the transcendental ideality of time, according to which it is nothing at all if one abstracts from the subjective conditions of sensible intuition, and cannot be counted as either subsisting or inhering in the objects in themselves (without their relation to our intuition).[40]

Referring to the concept of space, for Kant, as well as the space and time, is not a concept but an intuition. It is an intuition, so a pure, a priori, non-empiric intuition. As a pure form of sensitivity space represents a condition for all external intuitions, a condition which is necessary to designate all relations, which settle in the intuited objects as being outside us. Space is not populated by objects or phenomena; it is only a representation, which makes possible the phenomenal constitution of all objects and of the ensemble of the reports between them, appearing as their subjective antecedents. Space is not an empiric concept because it cannot be taken out of the empiric intuitions. Space as such, in this perspective, is not built, it practically means not more limited spaces, which are prior represented, but it originally is non-mediated, as a unique and all-comprising space, the diverse of it being only a possibility, which thinking perceives as only later on, and this confirms again that space form the perspective of Kant is pure intuition. Therefore he draws

---

[39] Kant 2000, p. 162 (B46).
[40] Kant 2000, p. 164 (B52-A36).

several conclusions on the concepts of space by talking about a reality and ideality of space and the duality of reality:

> Our expositions accordingly teach the reality (i.e., objective validity) of space in regard to everything that can come before us externally as an object, but at the same time the ideality of space in regard to things when they are considered in themselves through reason, without taking account of the constitution of our sensibility. We therefore assert the empirical reality of space (with respect to all possible outer experience), through to be sure at the same time its transcendental ideality, that it is nothing as soon as we leave out the condition of the possibility of all experience, and take it as something that grounds the things in themselves.[41]

Kant's arguments on space and time have aroused a lot of controversy, the concepts being very complex. Thus, in his work, Kant has introduced several new words as sensation, appearance, matter, intuition or form, in order to identify the a priori elements of sensibility.

Going further we must say that Kant's remarks at the end of the metaphysic deduction of the categories, which present the table of the 12 categories[42], consist in the fundamental idea according to which self conscience is the one which insures the unity of categories.

SPACE AND TIME. HEIDEGGER'S MEDITATION

At the beginning of the 20th century, the works of Martin Heidegger had a major impact on the thinkers of the century. To support our statement, we should remember what Timothy Clark wrote:

> Martin Heidegger is the hidden master of modern thought. His influence on thinkers in the second half of the twentieth century, though often unspoken, is all pervasive, especially in that melange in the humanities known curiously as 'theory'. Heidegger's work touches the deepest, usually unconsidered assumptions of all work of thought, forming a reassessment of the drive to knowledge itself.[43]

The initial space represents the space of life, the everyday world being a world populated by objects, through which according to Heidegger, the Dasein[44] organizes its existence. In his work, only because man has always been

---

[41] Kant 2000, p. 160 (B44-A28).
[42] Kant 2000, pp. 212-213.
[43] Clark 2002, p. 1.
[44] Inwood 1999, pp. 42-44. Michael Inwood gives the definition of the word Dasein on three pages, trying to explain its meaning. From this we would like to extract some of the passages that we found to be important: „Mark Twain complained that some German words

in the world, the space of the world is possible. For the German philosopher space is not in subject, and the world is not in space, and space does not have the a priori structure from Kant.

Heidegger's most important task was to make sense of our existence. Thus, he claims that our existentiality lies a priori, but not space, just our existence. The term we know from Kant's works, to whom a priori knowledge was that what was known prior to any experience. The first a priori existential for Heidegger is being-in-the-world, and the next from the series and the order of his analysis are important.[45]

In *Being and Time,* Heidegger sees the world's spatiality as a condition of concrete possibility, trying to get away from the classic alternation objective space - subjective space.

Important for what we are trying to argue in this book is Heidegger's topic about the death or art. This topic is discussed by the German phylosopher in his work entitled *The Origin of the Work of Art*, which is seen as a radical paper on aesthetics. As Timothy Clark argued,

> The text explicitly rejects the terms that usually dominate discussion of this kind. It refuses to speak of art in terms of 'form' and 'content', 'individual creativity', 'meaning', 'artist's intention', 'aesthetic experience' or 'aesthetic judgement' or 'taste'. The essay is a rejection of the Western tradition of aesthetics and a retrieval of its forgotten sources.[46]

---

seem to mean everything. One such word is *da.* It means 'there' ('There they go') and 'here' ('Here they come'), as well as 'then', 'since', etc. Prefixed to *sein*, 'to be' it forms *dasein,* 'to be there, present, available, to exist'. (…) He revives the original sense, 'being there', often writing *Da-sein* to stress this. *Dasein* is essentially in the WORLD, and lights up itself and the world. (…) It does not locate man's essence in some specific faculty such as reason: one of Dasein's central features, along with THROWNNESS and FALLING, is EXISTENCE, and this means that it has to decide how to be, and is not essentially and inevitably rational. (…) Later, man is distinguished more sharply from *Dasein. Dasein* is not man, but a relationship to being diat man acquires and may lose. Man may be simply a SUBJECT or a rational animal. Moreover *Da-sein* is 'between' man and the gods rather than coincident with man himself".

[45] Gelven 1989, pp. 58-59. Michael Gelven wrote: „Scientifically, the fact that I am on the planet earth (world) in not *a priori*: it is learned only through experience. But the fact that, as Dasein, I must have a world to live in, to dwell in, to call my home, *is a priori*. What is meant by this Being-in, if not the simple space-time location of physics? (…) A human being, then, is one who exists in such a way as to belong to this earth – i.e., a *human* being is an earth being in the sense of having a home here. It *belongs*. (…) The real meaning behind this existential is that my *surroundings* (*Umwelt:* <<environment>>) are not simply *there*, but they affect me and I them. I cannot think of myself as existing simply as a space-time locus".

[46] Clark 2002, p. 41.

For Heidegger, art[47] is not a matter of representation, and in his essay, architecture plays a special role, being something that does not represent anything. The author clearly presents this by describing the Greek temple:

> A building, a Greek temple, portrays nothing. It simply stands there in the middle of the rock-cleft valley. The building encloses the figure of the god, and in this concealment lets it stand out in the holy precinct through the open portico. (...) The temple and its precinct, however, do not fade away into the indefinite.[48]

As Clark argued, the presence of architecture and it's usage to provide shelter, opens the space, which in fact is the world, for peope to dwell and to be able to ask themselves questions and to provide answers and understanding of the surrounding reality.[49] For Heidegger, architecture isn't just built anywhere, the space it is constructed upon is priviledged, and architecture itself is what makes that space to become a place, to become visible for everybody. Thus, the place (Ort in Deutsch) is not just any place, is exactly what stands for the existance of the place itself, what Heidegger refers to as Stätte.

In *The Origin of the Work of Art*, Heidegger refers to an existance where the World and the Earth upholds each other and in the same time create a tension between them. Thus, the tension is presented as the reluctance between something that opens and another thing that closes. The world is the openness to decisions and the earth is the exit from ourselves and the refuge therewith.

Heidegger also had three significant writings on architecture[50] and

---

[47] Inwood 1999, pp. 18-19. Michael Inwood gave the definition ot the terms art and th work that Heidegger used and we will give some paragraphs: „The work of art is more like a PROJECT, which sets up a world in which choices can be made. Truth, die [the] revelation of being, is 'set into the work' and 'set to work', illuminating die [the] world and die [the] EARTH on which it rests. As DASEIN is drown in its own project and understands itself in terms of it, so die [the] artist is originated by the work of art. The point is not simply that no one is an artist until he creates a work, but diat [that] the artist is not in control of his own creativity, art is a sort of impersonal force diat [that] uses the artist for its own purpose".

[48] Heidegger 1971 cited Clark 2002, p.45.

[49] Clark 2002, pp. 45-46. Thimothy Clark wrote: „the fact that architecture provides basic shelter already suggests the profound seriousness of art in general for Heidegger, as opening the space in which people dwell and understand things. Art here is not considered as a realm of cultural achievement, or the basis for a canon of great monuments or examples of 'creativity', nor as a manifestation of the human spirit, nor as an historical document of unusual interest, nor as a cultural force either supportive or subversive of dominant ideologies. Heidegger sees the essential power of art – stifled in the modern world – as the setting up of the overall 'world' within which and after which all these other views of art could alone become thinkable".

[50] Those three writings were: *The Thing* (1950), *Building Dwelling Thinking* (1951) and *...poetically, Man dwells...* (1951) and were written after the end of the Second World War, when

They approach related questions in similar ways. Each text amplifies the thinking of the others. In all three, he chose to explore an aspect of contemporary existence that indicated an unfavourable comparison with the past as he saw it, offering a tragic view of contemporary human experience.[51]

We will make a short presentation of the main concepts and ideas from those three works of Heidegger, that are important mostly not just because of the questions being raised, but also because those are the first essays to be lectured after his long silence. Each of this essay is dense and complex and are created in the authors characteristic circular type. An important issue raised by the author was about the shrinking distances in the post-war era. Those writings were very well described by Adam Sharr, and a full analyse of these papers would take the entire space dedicated for this book. Thus, we will only try to present what is most important out of the phylosopher's entire work. What is most important to continue our argument is his statements on place and space. Thus, in *Building Dwelling Thinking* we are being clearly notified even from the start about the main purposes of the essay:

> In what follows we shall try to think about dwelling and building. This thinking about building does not presume to discover architectural ideas, let alone to give rules for building. This venture in thought does not view building as an art or as a technique of constructions; rather it traces building back into that domain to which everything that *is* belongs.[52]

In his essay, the phylosopher completed his argument by giving examples of a bridge and a farmhouse, in order to explain the concept of place. Thus, in his construction of the argument, he states that a space comes into existence only because of the bridge is there:

> Thus the bridge does not first come to a location to stand in it; rather, a location comes into existence only by virtue of the bridge.[53]

Furthermore, he continues his argumentation on the concept of space, as follows:

> Only things that are locations in this manner allow for spaces. What the word for space, *Raum, Rum,* designates is said by its ancient meaning. *Raum* means a place cleared or freed for settlement and lodging. A space is something that has

---

in Germany there was undergoing a massive program for reconstruction.
[51] Sharr 2009, p. 22.
[52] Heidegger 1971, p. 145. An online copy of Heidegger's essay *Building Dwelling Thinking* from Heidegger, M., 1971. *Poetry, Language, Thought*. London: Harper & Row, 143-161.Document accsessed online on the Scribd.com webpage at the address: http://www.scribd.com/doc/30495822/Heidegger-Poetry-Language-Thought on 5th of august 2010 at 7:56 PM.
[53] Heidegger 1971, p. 154.

been made room for, something that is cleared and free, namely within a boundary. (…) *Accordingly, spaces receive their being from locations, and not from „space"*. Things which, as locations, allow a site we now in anticipation call buildings. They are so called because they are made by a process of building construction. Of what sort this making – building – must be, however, we find out only after we have first given thought to the nature of those things which of themselves require building as the process by which they are made.[54]

In the following paragraphs, the author tries to make a distinction between space and place and to answer the legitimate question

Fore one thing, what is the relation between location and space? For another, what is the relation between man and space?[55]

For a comprehensive understanding, Adam Sharr's[56] argument is very useful, as he discusses the importance of the good translation of the words and what they mean in English and German. Thus, places are spaces appreciated through human experience and use, and this is why a certain space is chosen by the builder to build and it becomes a place.

Furthermore, we inevitably came to the matter of place identification. For Heidegger, the most important instance for the creation of the bridge is the way the builder has chosen the place for the (hypothetical) bridge to be built. This is the most crucial moment[57], and after the creation of the building (or any other type of construction) the place will be remembered and people will understand it as the place of the bridge. Regarding place identification, Heidegger refers in his writing, as an example, to a picnic table: how people will choose the place to lay the blanket, how the blanket will be arranged, how the food will be arranged on the blanket. All these imply place identification.[58]

---

[54] Heidegger 1971, p. 154.
[55] Heidegger 1971, p. 155.
[56] Sharr 2009, pp. 51-57.
[57] Sharr 2009, p. 53. Adam Sharr wrote: „Whatever it might be termed, this is for Heidegger the moment that dwelling is inscribed in place through building. There would have been reasons, in Heidegger's story, why the builder chose the particular spot on the bank. Perhaps undulations of river and bank were conducive to building there. Perhaps it was the easiest spot to defend from invaders. Whatever the reason, it was judged the most appropriate spot to place a bridge. (…) The initial identification of place was, through building, adopted by others and absorbed into their understanding".
[58] Sharr 2009, p. 54. Adam Sharr wrote: „For Heidegger, this example wouldn't be trivial. It illustrates activities of place identification which, to him, remained constantly in play, shaping the organisation of rooms, buildings, towns and cities. In this Heideggerian scheme, the choices which locate a house in a landscape are not so different to those involved in arranging a picnic blanket in a park. If a house is located and built in such a landscape, outbuildings might later be configurated around it, involving other identifications of place. In time, a

The works of Heidegger are very complex and they proved to be useful in our research on the concept of cultural landscape. We know that it is almost like a virus. More you read on this matter, harder it is to finally get to a point. It is in the same circular manner of the philosopher, when questions are always answered with another question. Is like it is never finished, there is always something to write about Heidegger. And is fascinating. Therefor, we will end our presentation of his most important concepts (for our research) as follows:

> Man's relation to location, and through location to spaces, inheres in his dwelling. The relationship between man and space is none other than dwelling, strictly through and spoken. When we think, in the manner just attempted, about the relation between location and space, but also about the relation of man and space, a light falls on the nature of the things that are locations and that we call buildings.[59]

Thus, the dependency on spatial perception of time is closely bound to the passivity of the subject and his activities towards certain temporal interiorities. We must take into consideration a returning of the sensitivity, a new beginning in the configuration of the social, the solution to the passivity and the lack of cohesion of the subject in the social life by the accent on becoming and relations through the affirmation of the difference between the subjects.

---

neighbouring house might be added, then another house, a street, another street, then a village and over time a town or even a city. Cities, especially if not planned, might be said to record many milions of place identifications in their layout, most of them long forgotten like the people who made them and the reasons for which they were made. (...) The world, for Heidegger, is parcelled up into interesting places of many sorts, sizes, shapes and scales; identified by individuals and kept to themselves or shared. Gloriously, according to the philosopher's outlook, activities involving the identification of place are neither logical nor systematic; remaining subjective, tentative, shifting and contingent".

[59] Heidegger 1971, p. 158.

Language, society and identity. A cultural landscape perspective

Language related to our research. Short introduction

We must admit that human language is something unique and special. Is what makes us different in a way from all the other living creatures on Earth. Thus, language and society are key concepts in social theory, and as argued later in this book, language is a key component of a cultured landscape. In our research on this subject, we have found several different ways of referring to the connection between language and society. Some have linked the two concepts with ideology[60], others consider language as a marker of identity at a social level[61].

Before going further, we will refer to Heidegger's works one more time. *On the Way to Language* is the one that interests us the most. For the German philosopher is all about "undergoing an experience with the language"[62], about the relation between the speaker, language and word. The individual is bound to his language and is closely related to it. As Heidegger said,

> in order to be who we are, we human beings remain committed to and within the being of language, and can never step out of it and look at it from somewhere else. Thus we always see the nature of language only to the extent to which language itself has us in view, has appropriated us to itself.[63]

---

[60] Robson, Stockwell 2005, p. 8. Quote:"In thinking about the relationship of language to forms of social interaction, we need to think about the concept of ideology. Ideology was for some years a very unfashionable term, being associated with an unstable form of classical Marxism. Like the 'class struggle' or the 'proletariat', ideology was too clearly associated with an era which – with the fall of the Berlin Wall, the disintegration of the Soviet system, the 'end of history', the emergence of globalisation and 'the third way' – was left to bear little relation to the political terrain of the late twentieth and early twenty-first centuries".

[61] Edwards 2009, p. 21. Quote:"Language can certainly be considered as a 'marker' at the individual level. (…) But the importance of language as an identity marker at a group level is much more readily evident".

[62] Heidegger 2003, p. 57. Quote:"To undergo an experience with something – be it a thing, a person, or a god – means that this something befalls us, strikes us, comes over us, overwhelms and transforms us. When we talk of <<undergoing>> an experience, we mean specifically that the experience is not of our own making; to undergo here it means that we endure it, suffer it, receive it as it strikes us and submit to it. It is this something itself that comes about, comes to pass, happens".

[63] Heidegger 2003, p. 134.

Even so, the philosopher does not relate language directly to society at any level, but we can find in his works words like "awareness", "remoteness"[64], "neighbourhood", "earth", "world", and "sky". Thus, in the third lecture on *The Nature of Language,* while talking about nearness and remoteness with regard to the word and language, he comes to the meanings of space and time, and as he argues,

> when we intend nearness, remoteness comes to the fore. Both stand in a certain contrast to each other, as different magnitudes of our distance from objects.[65]

Language, written or spoken, has the great characteristic that through different ways of distribution, it connects individuals and communities. Language defines us. Thus, in cultural landscape studies, language is a particular component which refers to us in connection to ethnicity, religion, gender and beliefs. Language is unique. We express our ideas through it, we interact with each other, we define certain characteristics of the seen or unseen. We use it to talk about everything, not just what is present or past. Those characteristics are called displacement and open-endedness[66]. Nevertheless, language presents variations, mostly with regard to geographical places. These variations we call dialects. But these variations are also related to a spatial – temporal dimension that makes the nature of language as it is today. In order to understand this, we will quote Heidegger again:

> However, what has all this to do with the nature of language? More than our thinking can encompass today. We may of course have had an intimation by now, in the form of that positive system which reckons nearness and remoteness as measurements of distance in space and time conceived as parameters. (…) Even so, we are bound to insist that a certain spatial-temporal relatedness belongs to every neighbourhood.[67]

---

[64] Heidegger 2003, p. 102. Quote: "To the calculating mind, space and time appear as parameters for the measurement of nearness and remoteness, and this in turn as static distances. But space and time do not serve only as parameters; in this role, their nature would soon be exhausted – a role whose seminal forms are discernible early in Western thinking, and which then, in the course of the modern age, became established by this way of thinking as the standard conception".

[65] Heidegger 2003, p.102.

[66] Trask 2010, p.5. Quote: "Displacement is the use of language to talk about things other than the here and now. (…) Open-endedness is our ability to use language to say anything at all, including lots of things we've never said or heard before. (…) Both of these phenomena, our ability to talk about places and things far away in space and time, and our ability to produce and understand new utterances virtually without limit, are so familiar to us that we never give them a moment's thought. And yet they are truly remarkable. Remarkable – and absolutely vital".

[67] Heidegger 2003, p. 103.

Therefore, dialect is closely related to identity. The spatial-temporal condition determines the transformations of individuals, groups, communities and language itself, as every other aspect of human existence in a contemporary world. The term identity is quite ambiguous, but John Edwards has tried to shed some light on it:

> The essence of identity is similarity: things that are identical are the same, after all, and the word stems from the Latin *idem*. And this most basic sense is exactly what underpins the notion of identity as it applies to personality. (…) It signifies a continuity, in other words, that constitutes an unbroken thread running through the long and varied tapestry of one's life.[68]

After this short introduction, in the next sub-chapter, we will discuss on the topic of language, society, and identity as being an important parameter of cultural landscape studies.

LANGUAGE AS A BINDER

In the philosophy of culture we make the distinction between the actual culture and civilization. Thus culture is a profound education of man, and civilization an improvement of the means and conditions outside its life. Civilization is no entity which opposes to culture, but it is only one of its aspects. Considering the above mentioned, we can define culture under anthropological and ethnological aspect as being

> the way of life of a people, seen in its integrity, as a system of attitudes, values, ideas, conducts and institutions,[69]

having an explicit reference to the ethnic frame.

We can define the contemporary period as a period of great challenge for the intellect, a period in which conscience, as it has been understood till then, radically changes its significance, suddenly becoming an effect, thus being degraded. Postmodernism, as a way of thinking, appeared as the only possible way to continue, once with the disappearance of metaphysics, with the secularization of new concepts and, different types to set the problem were born. Self-conscious automatically becomes a conscience of something, the being can no longer be reduced to concept, so that quite before the actual

---

[68] Edwards 2009, p. 19.
[69] Georgiu 1997, p. 206.

birth of Postmodernism the idea of deconstructions appears once with phenomenology (starting with Husserl and continuing with Martin Heidegger).

The unique, individual conscience isn't unaltered and unaffected living somehow broken from the real, but is from the first contact of the individual with the surrounding world, altered by the word, so by the exterior. The word has existed since the world. The conscience belongs to each person, while the word belongs to everybody. All individuals who belong to a culture, who talk the same language, use the same words. The words are thus entities which circulate between individuals, which they take and give a sense according to his powers. Thus we can see the word as a binder of interpersonal communication and at the same time as a symbol. The word binds people using a language and makes possible the apparition of a community. J.F Lyotard writes that:

> The self is a small thing, but it is not isolated, but caught in a texture of more complex and more mobile relation than ever. It is always situated, either young or old, man or woman, rich or poor, in <<knots>> of communication circuits, as intimate as they may be.[70]

Community is bound both by cultural aspects and technical aspects, by situations which individuals have to confront together and by their common culture actions, meaning both material components and non-material components. Thus a local identity can appear. A local identity does not exist without people. Where there are no people we can talk only about local specific as certain characteristics of a place, with particularities.

But since the post-modern epoch the problem of the idea of identity brought by the change, which takes place at the level of a paradigm has been set. As Grigore Georgiu says:

> The new way of philosophical representation of the relation universality and peculiarity prepared by the convergence of different spiritual experiences is completely different from the instrumented one[71]

The identity of a community, nation or region is a dynamic process which belongs to all types of relations existing at the level of that community, which are either from the modern period or not, because there have always been interpersonal relations. It is obvious that they differed from epoch to epoch, and now in this post-modern and technicalized period the types of relations are different and varied, because in a way even the purposes for which individuals communicate have changed; today people can communic-

---
[70] Lyotard 2003, p. 37.
[71] Georgiu 1997, p. 83.

ate in ways and over distances which were unimaginable not long time ago. We thus unknowingly pass from a world where cultural isolation ruled to a world where intercultural factors rule, from an era characterized by the cultural autonomy of traditional isolated groups to an era of the generalization of inter-relations and communications.

There has to be mentioned the fact that there is no identity except culture, but there is culture outside identity. Consequently cultural identity proposes making aware of the belonging to a culture and making aware of the local or regional identity can be done only at the moment of cultural production, at the moment of creation. Where there is no faith in progress, no culture as a form of human activity can be produced. A cultural creation results from the faith that there still are unsolved themes.

On the same level we can say about a culture which can give forms of local identity that it is

> a dowry of conceptions, habits, faiths, customs, values and appreciations, structures and forms, everything that human groups, peoples and nations have created and kept in order to be transmitted form generation to generation. And between the individual identity and the anthropological identity there is an endless row of relative possible identities. Along history among these cultures there were changes and contaminations in a movement like the Brown on, but which created force lines (...) which concentrated power energies of high drainage.[72]

This is as life itself is growth and diminution, a kind of force game between a force and a counter-force. Life itself is growth and diminution. If the force balance were perfect, there would be no full life, living but there would be a soulless entity, a thing like everything else in the surrounding world.

Talking about these two competing forces we have to mention Foucault who takes Nietzsche's idea of will of power and reinterprets it as will of knowledge. For Nietzsche life is will of power because, if we pay attention to how life functions, we will notice the will of power and the elementary tension, which through the existence of an unequal force leads to the apparition of force game. And the will of power is the force game of creation and destruction, because it is a will to dominate in you so that the creative forces should get to dominate the destructive forces.

We can say that a local identity can be formed through speech, so through language, so through the word. Because the world has a meaning and can be understood only when individuals give meanings to the words through which

---

[72] Matei 2004, p. 29.

they describe the surrounding world (they can not be identical, as each individual can understand a word differently from another individual).

Speech is the concrete manifestation of language. Language is the minimum request for a society to be called society, for a community to exist, because there is a need of common things which should keep people together, in which they could find themselves, so that we can talk about a national, local or regional identity. If there were nothing in common there would be no society. Talking about the nature of social legislation Lyotard notes in *Postmodern condition*:

> but in order to admit the idea that language games are the minimum of relation for a society to exist, we do not have to resort to a Robinsonade: before birth through the very name it gets, the child is placed in the position of referent of history, which those around him relate and in relation to which he will later evolve. Or simpler: the issue of social bound, as an issue, is a language game (...); this issue already is a social bound.[73]

People need this power of integration; they need social recognition and the bound between them at the level of the social. People need language, and even more, they need its rules. Because, if we looked upon language as a social game, any game would need some rules (for example specific languages used in different domains or in different society frames - church, school, family, etc.).

Language evolved from the strictly oral expression to the written word, first to facilitate the transmission of messages and then out of the inner need to build a common binder. Thus stories appeared which were a way of conveyance and conservation of the common memory creating the frames of common local identity. This language and its evolution belong to a tradition. A tradition can be defined as the influence of anterior cultural work on the present one. Tradition is formed through what we call education. Culture creators are transmitted the materials and means which are used by the cultural creation through education. This can be of different ways, from the education received from the family, the social frame and then from schools, as I mentioned earlier. Education has the purpose to prepare us for solving life tasks. The conclusion of what has been written so far can be that tradition can be considered one of the important conditions for producing cultural aspects. This is a necessary force, but only when it is in balance with freedom and innovation.

---

[73] Lyotard 2003, pp. 37-38.

Words form sentences and then compound sentences, discourses, which are built according to certain rules which in time become patterns by often repetitions and modifications. Then other people are guided by them in order to formulate what they want to express, as Foucault said

> Language has in itself its inner principle of proliferation.[74]

But these frames are fluctuant, they change from time to time as society changes, so we can talk about an open language, about a

> absolutely opne dimension of a language which can no longer stop, because in a definite speech it will never say the truth only from a future discourse, entirely consecrated to expressing what will have already said.[75]

By its nature it develops the spiritual identity of several individuals who live together between the same spatial and temporal coordinates. We could say that language is a way of instrument with inter-subjective value. People use language to communicate and thus they create bounds with their fellow people.

One of the ways people created a common binder, through which they managed to know each other and build something proper for the community they were living in for their region, their status and, broader, their living area were stories. Lyotard is the one who gives examples of the way in which stories in their different forms throughout history have had an important role for the individual. Thus, popular stories have been created as an example for the formation of an individual, for the way he chose to live his life, through examples of stories about success or failure of mythical heroes, which were fundamental for the power of the society they were living in.

Another advantageous part of narration is the fact that it permits language to be different, it permits different meanings.

> We could say that 'literature', as it was constituted and appointed in the modern age, manifests the re-apparition of the living part of language, in the 17th and 18th century, the proper existence of language, its old work solidarity registered in the world were dissolved in the functioning of representation; any language existed as a discourse. The art of language was a manner to 'note', at the same time to designate a thing and to set out signs around this thing.[76]

Last but not least the stories help transforming these language games into practice.

---

[74] Foucault 1996, p. 82.
[75] Lyotard 2003, p. 93.
[76] Foucault 1996, p. 86.

> The knowledge these narrations render, far from attaching only the enunciation functions, determines thus at the same time what we have to say in order to be correctly understood, to listen in order to be able to speak and what we have to interpret (...) to make the object of a story.[77]

But a society where these language games are obvious is a fragmentary society, which can no longer be set in the old (classical) sociologic classifications.

The stories and language that belong to them make possible the inter-human communication helping the individual evolve and develop, the narration being one of the possible manifestations of the human spirit in the wish to develop. Through stories, people belonging to the present societies form not only a vision upon the world but also social bounds. And the fact that these stories and narrations are always being read makes, according to Lyotard, them to create social bounds which people need. We can linguistically observe different understanding frames from the systematic form of language which is language to the talking act, which is the concrete and daily manifestation of this language.

Then, with time, together with the evolution of research and education, we need new types of social relations, which should cope with the present, the reality. For Lyotard knowledge is of two kinds, both narrative and scientific, which for him from the perspective of language are of the same kind, but the narrative knowledge does not need any rules as strict as the scientific one, meaning that they are in opposition. Lyotard says that

> scientific knowledge can not know and can not make to know that it is the real knowledge without the other knowledge, the story, which for it is non-knowledge.[78]

Regarding the way in which life exists and what maintains the inter-human relations, Michel Foucault speaks about the way in which life (biologically speaking) is characterized by power relations. From this perspective the object of power becomes life itself, where it does not matter who exercises power but who manages to resist and support it. These relations configure the map of relations between the individuals, especially in this post-modern time where we can talk only about local identities, surpassing the limits of the countries, the states, the nations. Foucault says:

> We observe that the experience of language belongs to the same archaeological net as the knowledge of nature's things. To know these things means to em-

---

[77] Lyotard 2003, p. 46.
[78] Lyotard 2003, p. 56.

phasize the system of assemblies, which made them close and solitary one against the other; but similitude could not be noticed only to the extend that an assembly of signs at their surface formed the text of an obvious indication.[79]

In conclusion, as from the perspective of the human sciences, we can say that man is devised passing from individual as an object of study of the language sciences, to the language itself as an object of study, the same we can say that there was a passing from understanding the individuals within a country which gives its measure to their understanding as proper individuals in a world in which geographical borders are more and more flexible, where the perception of vicinity and spatiality is different, in an era of total globalisation (from geographical, to economical, cultural or linguistic).

---

[79] Foucault 1996, p. 82.

TRACING THE CONCEPT OF CULTURAL LANDSCAPE

TOWARDS MODERNITY: MODERNISM AND THE INTER-WAR ARCHITECTURE

The modern movement in architecture[80], which appeared at the beginning of the 20th century, represented an answer to the changes in the technological development, society and the science of materials. Thus the new world of machines determined the adopting of a new thinking among the artists of the time, which led to the change of the way in which we perceive life and the environment and the way in which we actively participate. Thus the modernist ideas penetrated into graphics, design, and architecture, influencing art, literature and music of those times.

The term modernism derives from the Latin modernus, meaning recent and appears in opposition to traditionalism at the end of the 19th century and the beginning of the 20th century, being a cultural, artistic and ideatic movement and was represented by: constructivism, cubism, Dadaism, expressionism (abstract), fauvism, functionalism, futurism, surrealism, Bauhaus, De Stijl, the International Style, etc. Together with this term we meet also the term modernity, which is different from modernism, deriving from it and representing an artistic movement influenced by mankind's progresses through industrialization, technologization and mechanization, doubting the previous philosophical principles and exploration through art (more on this you will find in the following chapter). In close connection the term of modern architecture refers to the edifices which adopt simplified and resembling stylistic forms by eliminating the ornament. Some architecture historians connect modern architecture with modernity and thus with the enlightenment, as a result of the social and political revolutions, and others consider that this is the result of technological and engineering development in close relation

---

[80] Ballantyne 2004, p. 24. Quote: „Architecture is produced when buildings and minds meet, and the stories we tell about architecture are as much about minds as they are about buildings – our own minds come into the picture, as well as other people's. When Pyrs Gruffudd points out that the sky was once a part of an <<RAF pastoral>>, he is not claiming that the sky is architecture, but there is a similar process at work when we see honesty and virtue in traditional vernacular architecture, or suppose that a Modernist building expresses the spirit of our age. In all this cases an <<object>> comes into contact with a mental apparatus, and is configured in such a way as to be culturally significant".

with the discovery of new materials of construction such as steel, iron and glass. Modernity is a term, which refers to the modern epoch, different from modernism including the period between 1630 and 1940. But to finish this discussion on modernity and modernism, will take a very long time and space and is already a topic very much discussed by many critics and theorists.

Thus, the problem of modernism in architecture was not of (re)transmitting a culture of well-known architectural forms, but promoting the experiments and (re)inventions in this field. Modernism became academic from its beginning, but the affirmation forms are different. Cubism, futurism, expressionism, constructivism or De Stijl had as a directive principle the change of creative techniques of the past, being often encouraged by Marxism and anarchism, the avant-garde considering that the radical techniques applied in art are messengers of a new life style. The modern movement can be considered a revolutionary one by the trial to break the existing barriers at that time between aesthetics, technology and society, to produce constructions of a functional visual quality for citizens. Their vision proposed adopting universal projecting solutions, which should satisfy life standards of citizens and which should embrace the universal principles of aesthetics such as: using the volume and the transparency against mass and ornament, the steadiness of composition against symmetry as well as the implication of a technological refinement in the process of construction.

Adopting new architecture programs by architects, the structural sincerity by leaving the apparent structure, the simplification of the ornament and even its elimination as well as the wish to get into the conscience of the public were the directive principles of the modern architecture. Thus, architecture reinvented itself, passed over the old principles becoming one of functionalistic thinking. At world level, at the beginning of the 1900's several international architects adopted new architecture solutions in order to integrate old traditional principles with new expressing ways specific to the new technology and materials. There are numerous examples such as Louis Sullivan and Frank Lloyd Wright in Chicago, Victor Horta in Bruxelles, Antoni Gaudi in Barcelona, Otto Wagner in Vienna and Charles Rennie Mackintosh in Glasgow. They tried to impose the *new* in their creation. The term modern had first appeared in a publication of those times, trying to announce a new beginning in architecture.[81] The English artist and poet William Morris was

---

[81] Otto Wagner, *Modern Architecture: a Guidebook for his Students to this Field of Art,* translated by Harry Mallgrave, appeared at the Anton Schroll publishing house, in 1902.

among the forerunners of the modernist ideology through his writings, which formed the base of the movement *Arts and Crafts*, which militated in favour of turning back to the manually created products, was against industrialization and mass production of the objects and considered that utility was as important as form. Another important figure, being considered the first modern architect, was Louis Henri Sullivan, the one who created the famous phrase „*Form ever follows Function*"[82], for whom functionalism meant the elimination of the ornament, thus the constructions being able to freely express the purpose for which they were created, based on the principle of projection from inside towards outside, leaving structure to dictate form and façade[83]. After 1920 two important figures of architecture adopted the industrial language: Walter Gropius and Le Corbusier. Gropius was the principle of the Bauhaus school whose declared purpose was to revolutionize art and architecture education by combing theory with practice, the projection with the very building of design objects. Gropius managed to combine art with technology, educating new generations of architects and designers, who should adopt the ideologies of the new modernist movement. Next to Gropius the Bauhaus school was led by important figures of those times such as Paul Klee, Lyonel Feininger, Wassily Kandinsky, Laszlo Moholy-Nagy and Marcel Breuer. Bauhaus had to confront with the educational system imposed by the French architecture school Beaux-Arts, a system which was considered a paradigm of the 19th century (and which had influenced the modern architecture thinking in Romania, as you will find out later in this chapter). Still, the two schools were based on resembling principles, such as the importance of function in the projection of buildings, the association and integration in the existing context and structural rationality and sincerity.

---

[82] Louis Henri Sullivan was considered the America's first modern architect. One of his famous quotes was: "It is the pervading law of all things organic, and inorganic, of all things physical and metaphysical, of all things human and all things super-human, of all true manifestations of the head, of the heart, of the soul, that the life is recognizable in its expression, that form ever follows function. This is the law". Cited from http://architecture.about.com/od/greatarchitects/p/sullivan.htm. Website accessed on 28th of September 2010, at 20.04 PM.
[83] Louis Henri Sullivan was very talented with regard to ornamentation. Besides his famous quote from before, another one is very important in order to understand architect's beliefs and intentions. Quote: "Ornament and structure were integral; their subtle rhythm sustained a high emotional tension, yet produced a sense of serenity. But the building's identity resided in the ornament. It was the spirit animating the mass and flowing from it, and it expressed the individuality of the building...". Cited from http://www.chicagohistory.org/sullivan150/about/ornament.php. Website accessed on 28th of September 2010, at 20.45 PM.

In France, Eugene Viollet-le-Duc proposed defining a new architectural style of the end of the 19th century, which was about to develop as a result of discovering new construction materials, and the movement Art Nouveau of the 1890's represented a trial to surpass stylistic traditions through a new approach, a new architecture with new principles. In his book *Space, Time and Architecture: The Growth of a New Tradition*, Sigfried Giedion managed to transpose the new architecture in a special cultural frame, sustaining the thesis according to which, looking at the architecture of the past times, we can observe how they reported to the future.[84] Giedion's book had a great influence among the young modernist architects, but it was known only in universities and in the close area of the profession.

Together with the modernist movement neither the history nor the theory of architecture remained uninfluenced, and known critics and historians such as Emil Kaufmann, Colin Rowe, Reyner Banham and Manfredo Tafuri influenced the modernist ideology. Derrida suggested that the borders of subjects such as architecture and history are of political nature, thus temporally delimitated or situated even in fictive temporalities, and Baudelaire was one of the promoters,

> insisting upon the lack of relevance of the past in perceiving the present.[85]

Baudelaire affirmed a series of characteristics of modernity, among which we have to mention the fragmentary, the insignificance and the autonomy. The fragmentary has always been an element of the critics towards the modernists because they (the artists) were painting details and impressions. The insignificance implied the disappearance of meaning, meaning that

> the work doesn't want to say anything.[86]

Autonomy represented the Baudelaire's definition of modernity, of the dual nature of the beauty, which imposed the artist a critical conscience:

---

[84] Giedion 2002, p. xliii. Quote:" I have always regarded the past as something not dead but an integral part of existence, coming to understand more and more the wisdom of the Bergsonian saying that past gnaws incessantly into the future. It all depends on how oen approaches the past. One way is to regard it as a useful dictionary from which one can select forms and shapes. (…) The creative artists of the period – poets, painters, sculptors and architects – have taken another way. In their work, past, present, and future merge together as the indivisible wholeness of human destiny".
[85] Compagnon 1998, p. 35.
[86] Compagnon 1998, p. 33.

it is the very condition of modernity, which does not recognize the existence of the space exterior to art, of a code or subject and which consequently has to form the rules, the models and the critics itself.[87]

Thus the idea of architectural autonomy appeared pretty often in the modern period, being a leitmotiv since the 19th century, being in close connection to the wish to define the role of the architect in a world in which architectural qualities were classified according to *form* and *style*. Starting with Adolf Loos and continuing with Le Corbusier and Mies van der Rohe, the role of architecture and of the architect was laid on at the bases of the architectural autonomy in the modernist practice. Among all the architecture theorists, who have written about the autonomy of architecture, Emil Kaufmann has always been a reference name.[88] His thesis affirmed that modernism appears for the first time in architecture in the work of Claude Nicolas Ledoux in 1770 and reaches the climax with Le Corbusier in 1900's. Kaufmann introduced the notion of neoclassicism was the first to write about Ledoux, influencing many generations of young architects. He contested the origins of modernism and interrogated in his works nature and the way of abstracting in relation with the geometric forms seen at the representatives of the Enlightenment and the modern avant-guard, thus contesting the premises of anachronism in history and criticism. His work

> opened up the imbricated problems of form and politics, architecture and society, in a way that directly challenged the cultural ideology of National Socialism in the 1930s.[89]

For Kaufmann the general concept of "architectural autonomy" was the one of formal modifications of buildings, and the first and fundamental step, which represented the first change from Baroque till then, was the separation of buildings in relation with the functions they had.

Colin Rowe's interpretation of modernism was auto-reflexive and was searching for formal models in history, which he then interpreted and understood as formal procedures to permit him investigate the differences and similarities between the periods. It was shown both by Le Corbusier as well as by Marcel Breuer, that modernism was a „double edged machine".[90] On the one hand everything was submitted to a modernism of the form using the techniques of cohabitation serving the avant-garde ideologies, where a form-

---

[87] Compagnon 1998, p. 34.
[88] Emil Kaufmann is known for tracing the phrase "architecture parlante", that represents a concept of buildings that explain their own identity and function, to Claude Nicolas Ledoux.
[89] Vidler 2008, p. 20.
[90] Vidler 2008, p.104.

al strategy had to produce a new social order, and on the other hand modernism was looking for an eternal relation with society based on the abstracting of the traditional and the generalization of Classicism's principles.

Reyner Banham, engineer and art critic, was not at all convinced that the modern language of architecture would have consumed its resources at the end of the 1920's. In his work *Theory and Design in the First Machine Age*[91] he argued that the very formalist and academic limitations of this language led to a deadlock of the modern movement which substantiated the aspirations to invent a new architecture as a answer to the new social conditions and technological evolutions of the beginning of the 20th century.

Between 1920 and 1930 the *international style* appeared, whose name has its origins in the book of Henry-Russel Hitchcock and Philip Johnson, which presented the International Exhibition of Modern Architecture held in New York in 1932, The International Style intended to define a series of principles, which would characterize modern architecture, thus identifying three issues: expressing volume against mass, the balance of composition against the preconceived symmetry the total exclusion of the ornament. In Europe, the adepts of this style were Victor Horta and Henry van de Velde in Belgium, Antoni Gaudi in Spain or Otto Wagner in Austria. After 1920 we can name as adepts of the International Style the movement de Stijl of Denmark, Deutscher Werkbund and Bauhaus in Germany, or Le Corbusier in France. The creations of these European architects but also those overseas have always followed the ideals and forming principles of the style, and the already

---

[91] Banham 1960, p. 14. Quote: "While a series of revolutionary gestures around 1910, largely connected with the Cubist and Futurist movements, were the main point of departure for the development of Modern architecture, there were also a number of particular predisposing causes that helped to guide the mainstream of development into the channels through which it flowed in the Twenties. (...) The attitude of those who were to become the masters of Modern architecture to these traditions from the past was apt to be equivocal. The Werkbund and its members were the object of suspicion in some quarters, though most of the younger architects accepted the moral imperatives bound up in it. The Rationalist attitude was held in high regard, yet effectively repudiated by most of them, and the academic tradition was generally vilified, yet many of the ideas it embodied were taken over by them. The last circumstance makes the evaluation of Guadet's contribution to modern theory difficult to assess. Those who rejected the academic discipline did so because they felt it to be hostile to their conception of architecture, which they held to be functional, scientific and divorced from stylistic considerations".

known slogans „ornament is a crime"[92], „truth to materials"[93], „form follows function"[94] were statutory arguments of architecture creations.

In the above presented context architects of Romania try to range to the international current proving receptivity and understanding. The existing situation in our country is best described by the architect Florea Stanculescu:

> our cities have this aspect too: half ... (Romanian style) and half ... (modern style). I think that the truth is neither on one side nor on the other nor in the middle.[95]

In the unification process of all Romanian provinces architecture and arts had an important role in forming a national idea in this pluralist landscape. Thus, in 1937 at the Universal Exhibition of Paris our country is present with a national pavilion designed by Duiliu Marcu, a royal pavilion which was in the vicinity of Germany's pavilion designed by Albert Speer and of the Stalinist one. The pavilion used for the main façade models of Roman imperial architecture (the Arch of Triumph), and in the inner court we were presented the image of a neo-Romanian porch with wood masts and monastery arches, and the adjacent restaurant proposed a post Art Deco style. We can thus observe

> the ambiguities of architecture with several speeds, such as the inter--war one in Romania.[96]

The inter-war architecture suffered because of a too large variety of orientations and stylistic search, with extensions of eclecticism and classic-made architecture, with different attitudes towards the sources of traditional inspiration, mainly also because of the situation of our country situated at the confluence between the Eastern and the Western culture, which it tried to synthesize through personal spirituality. The most important architects, who distinguished themselves in this period, were Ion Mincu, Marcel Iancu, Horia Creangă, Duiliu Marcu, Petre Antonescu, G. M. Cantacuzino and Octav Doicescu.

---

[92] Manifest of Adolf Loos.
[93] Doctrine of the modern archtiecture according to which materials had to be used so that they should express teh message and not hide teh properties.
[94] Words of the architect Louis Sullivan from 1896 appeared in the article „*The tall office building artistically considered*" in Lippincott's Magazine. The whole paragraph is: "It is the pervading law of all things organic and inorganic,Of all things physical and metaphysical,Of all things human and all things super-human,Of all true manifestations of the head,Of the heart, of the soul,That the life is recognizable in its expression,That form ever follows function. This is the law."
[95] Stanculescu 1935, pp. 13-14.
[96] Ioan 2002, p. 80.

After the creation of the national state in 1918, Romania becomes a country with very broad development perspectives, especially as the crises of 1929-1933 did not affect Romania so much as other states. In this period new construction technologies appear, especially the wide use of reinforced concrete. The spiritual potential of the new generation of architects will benefit of the contribution of the European cultural movements, when the French academism is adopted by the Romanian architecture school. The new formal language of modernist constructions is being foreseen by the simplicity of forms, by the carrying structure, which responds to the functional necessities and the elimination of the decorative elements. The prosperous economic situation of our country, with a society open to emancipation, permits the infiltration of the modernist current among young architects. Thus we can distinguish the difference between the avant-garde of the European modern architecture and the one in our country. For the Western people modern architecture meant the break from the past, while in Romania everything was based on new principles, which continued the old traditions of the popular architecture. The Romanian inter-war architecture evolved according to some aesthetic and functional principles, which were the engines of development such as: use of the rectangular forms with multiple intersections with curve surfaces, grading the perception through the use of curve forms in contrast with the severity of rectangular forms; the horizontality of facades and the alternating with vertical elements marked through the release of some volumes, the use of the specific language for the exemplification of the composition; pure volumes, their accuracy and formal simplicity of the constructions are tightly connected with the force and refinement of the Romanian popular architecture. The total functional flexibility of the Eastern architecture will never be reached in our country although the plans of the buildings had suffered a series of formal adaptations.

The Romanian society was open and receptive to the modern movement, the new type of architecture, which resulted from the sketches of architects, being easily assimilated. The expression of the modernist current in architecture in our country was not a copy of the currents launched in the rest of Europe, passing through a filter of the personal culture, which benefited from a different and independent process of creation. In our country there were no groups of architects in different forms such as De Stijl, Deutscher Werkbund or Bauhaus, but the modernist stage of history proved to be most fertile in our cultural history, the modern architecture having an indisputable contribution to the transformation Romania passed though.

From modernity to the concept of cultural landscape

We must take into consideration that the study of a concept considered by many people as being post-modern, ambiguous and complicated in essence, will contain theories from a varied area of subjects, and the confusion the subtitle could create by joining the terms modernity and cultural landscape must be removed. We considered the use of the term modernity in the subtitle as the most appropriate, as we will use concepts and theories that had been produced at the beginning of the twentieth century.

Post-modernism criticized a series of concepts of modernity and launched at the same time new (or renewed) notions and terms, which define the environmental realities. These were easily assimilated in speeches and became almost usual notions, but whose meaning and signification are extremely complex. Two of such terms, which are important for our research, are those of cultural and city landscape. Even if for most the term of cultural landscape became like a manifestation of the politics, it first appeared in the work of Carl Ortwin Sauer. The concept of cultural landscape today suffered a series of enrichments and transformations, being much more complex than the one launched by Sauer, containing besides the material component also a mental component. We thus find the acquired character of culture as well as the process character, a process of attribution and (re)production, through which culture is an instrument in the study and analysis of the complexity of the contemporary societies, being a speech through which the social theories made in cultural terms get a greater load and represent an engine in the human activity and mind.

Thus, we perceive modernity in relation to the social-economic and social-cultural aspects imposed to man by the modernization process. It is a varied experience, which implies a brake from the past and traditions through the daily life in the urban or rural environment. In order to defend the presented ideas, we mention Hilde Heynen, who considered that

> modernity refers to the typical features of modern times and to the way that these features are experienced by the individual: modernity stands for the attitude towards life that is associated with a continuous process of evolution and

transformation, with an orientation toward a future that will be different from the past and from the present.[97]

The authoress affirms that modernity is a bipolar, objective and at the same time subjective phenomenon, those two aspects referring to the economic and social processes and to the artistic activities, personal experiences of the individual and cultural theories.[98] The spatial - temporal compression determined the complex transformation of the parameters of the human condition, which lead to a ramification and polarization of it, and the society relates to the evolution level of civilization, and in this whole picture the cities represent centers connected to different realities, opening the path of vast opportnities. It is known that cities have been from the beginning commercial centers, media centers and poles of the global policy, having a strategic role, which is much more important in the new globalization era.

Thus, the cultural landscape is a language of the modern society, which transmits the spiritual dimension of individuals, and the urban landscape is a cultural symbol, which expresses the values of the society, the city through its morphology being a medium through which these attributes are transmitted. Thus, the previous studies investigate the series of events and processes, which left their prints in the urban or rural morphology and the spatial structure of settlements, in order to be able to understand the factors, which lead to the emotional state of the individual in the urban frame and the quality of his life. Furthermore, modern studies on cultural landscape do have a tremendous influence from philosophy[99] in a subjective way, and the study wit-

---

[97] Heynen 1999, p. 10.
[98] Heynen 1999.
[99] Is about the use of human agency, the philosophical concept in the study of cultural landscape. A definition of human agency would be: „the capacity for human beings to make choices and to impose those choices on the world. It is normally deployed in contrast to natural forces, which are causes involving only unthinking deterministic processes, but in religion or theology occurs also as a counterpoint to the will of God. In this it is subtly distinct from the concept of free will, the philosophical doctrine that our choices are not the product of causal chains, but are significantly free or undetermined. Human agency entails the uncontroversial, lower claim that humans do in fact make decisions and enact them on the world. How humans come to make decisions, by free choice or other processes, is not at issue. Human agency invests a moral component into a given situation. If a situation is the consequence of human decision making, persons may be under a duty to apply value judgements to the consequences of their decisions, and held to be responsible for those decisions. Human agency entitles the observer to ask should this have occurred? in a way that would be nonsensical in circumstances lacking human decisions-makers." Definition was accsessed online on the website of WordiQ.com
http://www.wordiq.com/definition/Human_agency on the 3rd of august 2010 at 11:06 AM.

nessed multiple changes during the last one hundred years, since the beginning of the 20th century.[100]

The cultural landscape is the product of the inter-relation of space, a process being in a continuous change, on two sides and dynamic, its study being a difficult one, which implies a multi criterial and multi disciplinary analysis. The relation between the social structures and the urban, symbolic and utilitarian spaces is the one that can determine the interpretations of the cultural urban landscapes. The spaces and symbols of life in the urban environment are in relation to the economic, political and social ideologies and systems. The concept became a meta word of postmodern speeches about space and culture, being a social product of the scenery of urban life, which contains among buildings also spaces and different ways to express the cultural values and human behavior. The landscape as a system implies the connection of different aspects of human existence, thus creating a multidimensional and dynamic space for the contemporary urban life in which dualities of the type time/space, human/natural, present/past transform the cultural landscape into a speech of the complicity of relations.

Giovanni Maciocco treats two levels of the landscape perception for the modern man. The first level is represented by the concept of environmental image, a dynamic medium of the contemporary city, and the second level is about a counter-space of the metropolis.[101] At the symbolistical level the way of investigating the landscape is different, and from the cultural point of view, the landscape and its symbol are as subjective as possible. Such an analysis can refer only to the physical landscape, which has to be applied to the landscape as a representation. The landscape can be pretty often seen as a palimpsest. Thus, the symbol elements of the urban cultural landscape become icons of a local, regional and national identity. The recognition of this symbolic meaning of the landscape leads to assuming a political aspect of

---

[100] Whyte 2002, pp. 19-20. Ian Whyte wrote: „Subjective approaches to the study of landscape went through various shifts during the twentieth century. One, associated with modernism, tried to read the history of landscape mainly through the history of landscape painting. Another was linked with postmodernism. It removed the role of painting from centre-stage towards a semiotic and hermeneutic approach. Semiotics concerns the way in which signs are produced and given meaning, while hermeneutics includes the study fo interpretation and meaning, and treats landscapes as allegories fo psychological or ideological themes (...) Modern cultural landscape studies have focused on human agency, and on the social and economic processes underlying it, sometimes to the neglect of the physical environment, the role of which is often simplified and misunderstood. Many landscape changes caused by human activity are actually accomplished by physical processes operating at a speed or on a scale that is greater than normal".

[101] Maciocco 2008, p. 1.

space and to determining its mental and material qualities. The process of reading and decoding the landscape implies the finding of the hidden processes, which have formed it, and on which the existence of symbols is grounded. This methods determined a series of researchers to observe the landscape as a text, a social and cultural document, which while being read the levels of values and the processes were to be discovered, like some kind of reading through the lines.

No matter which of the concepts we are talking about, the urban landscape is composed of tensions and relations. Tensions, which include the distance and proximity of space, but, at the same time, also the relation between the two. The human mind and body are embraced by tensions in the process of observation or direct implication in the learning and reading of the urban landscape. Thus, the value systems and the ideologies are in direct relation with the permanent adaptation of social life, the individual being in a continuous search of identity in a urban space, which is continuously changing and in which the differentiation is the engine of evolution. The social events of the vast urban landscape are the ones, which give birth to new cultures or sub-cultures, which are different from the one, which already exist. This very difference led to the creation of the contemporary society, which transformed the city in a laboratory of diverse configurations, a space of representation, contestation and identification at the same time.

CULTURAL GEOGRAPHY AND THE BIRTH OF A FUNDAMENTAL CONCEPT

A possible trial to explain the term culture could be wrongly understood in a context in which the term cultural landscape represents the fundamental concept, which refers to almost everything that surrounds us, to a permanently changing and adapting reality. At the same time explaining culture could through our research in a completely wrong direction. We are interested in culture as a process of value creation, which through human activity led to modelling and changing the outer space. Thus, it is important to mention what Alexandru Tanase said in his studies of culture philosophy:

> no explicative point of view in culture could avoid reporting to two fundamental realities with which it is in correlation: nature and society.[102]

---

[102] Tanase 1968, p. 31.

We thus have a clear framing of the place that culture and nature have next to society, the three being connected and influenced one by the other, and the change of one leads to the change of adaptation of the others. Culture, associated to the term of landscape refers to a human field, which was modified by human intervention being called culture. Culture thus implies a creative impulse, the human spirit being implicated in a mental process. This mental side was ignored for a long time by geographers and theorists of culture while studying the cultural landscape, being introduced rather late, as a critique reaction to the first interpretations of the concept we today find fundamental.

Thus Don Mitchell presents the history of the apparition of the study of culture in geography because, as he says

> it is essential that we situate the history of <<culture>> in cultural geography within a social context – a context composed of changes both within the discipline and in the <<outside>> world.[103]

In Mitchell's vision everything started from the wish to understand the superiority of Western culture as it was considered at the beginning in Great Britain then in Germany and the United States. The author sustains that the roots of Anglo-American cultural geography are found in the theories of the 19th century of Great Britain and Germany, and in the first half of the 20th century the United States are to impose in this field, the father of the American cultural geography School being considered Carl Ortwin Sauer (1889-1975). The main directions which the cultural geography followed were in contradiction, first being considered environmental determinism, which had the purpose to bind the social behaviour of the individual with the components of the physical environment and secondly the studies about folklore, which tried to explain the cultural roots of contemporary civilization. This second aspect implies a cultural relativism, which was known mainly in anthropology, but which appeared in Sauer's works as well.

The theory of the environment is part of the material conditions of culture, as they were presented by Tudor Vianu. This theory was based on the fact that environment was considered a determinant factor in the way in which different cultures were connected with each other and were found in different geographical areas and the way in which the social behaviour of individuals was influenced by the environment. The theory's supporters sustained that

---

[103] Mitchell 2000, p.16. quote „it is essential that we situate the history of <<culture>> in cultural geography within a social context – a context composed of changes both within the discipline and in the <<outside>> world".

the environmental determiners as climate and different other geographic factors are the only responsible with the development of human culture and social condition. Tudor Vianu named the cosmic conditioning of culture reminding of writings of the 17th century, of Fontenelle and Montesquieu.[104]

In modern geography the first influences of environmental determinism in theory appear in the works of the German geographer Friedrich Ratzel, at the end of the 19th century, in which he launches the concepts of organic state and living space. His concepts appear after the well-known work of Charles Darwin *Origin of Species* in the year 1859 and were influenced by the evolution of biology, arguing that the state was organic (having in essence life) and that it need to grow in order to exist, thus existing a natural bound between the individual and the environment.

Around the 1920's environmental determinism crashed under the power of its own contradictions and irrelevances, and the end of the European colonialism made the political or economic expansion impossible. Thus redefining geography was tried, and Sauer's initiative to use culture theories in order to explain social differences has its roots in the German intellectualism as well, which was the base of the deterministic theory of the environment.

Furthermore, in order to understand and talk about structuralism it is essential to understand structure. We mention the fact that structure refers to mental models of concrete structures taken from reality. Models are not always evident and we need to understand some hidden or profound aspects, as Mark Glazer declared:

> The most difficult aspect of structuralism is that these structures are not based on concrete or physical phenomena as they are in biological or other sciences but based on cultural realities.[105]

Philosophic influences in the study of the cultural landscape are strongly coagulated around the thesis according to which the knowledge and the experience of the individual become the base of cultural ideas and social actions divided by the community and the way in which social experience influences thinking and the life of the citizen. Thus, the way we look upon the cultural landscape changes, passing from the status of passive entity to its active role in social, economic and political processed of the everyday life. In his folklore and vernacular architecture studies Henry Glassie refers to the intrinsic role of the opposition of order (control) and of chaos in all changes of the en-

---

[104] Vianu 1982, pp. 230-233.
[105] http://www.utpa.edu/faculty/mglazer/Theory/structuralism.htm accessed on 08.03.2010.

vironment, his argumentation being influenced by the structuralism of the anthropologist Claude Levi-Strauss who had

> the conviction that deep binary mental structures exist and are expressed and reinforced in ways of thinking about the world and human places within it.[106]

Glassie considered people, whatever their past and culture were, were building being guided by their ancestor's practices or the strictness of the laws of physics, but most of them were stimulated by their own experience in the built space. Thus, he mentioned architects, who, whatever their training was, had in their backgrounds memories of the inhabited space, of the seen images, of the lived experiences and of the touched material types. All these, together with the professional training[107], made an architect be a promoter of culture.

Jonathan Murdoch[108], in his trial to explain the main theories of poststructuralism in geography, considered it necessary, how to explain the term of structuralism, and afterwards to be able to explain post-structuralism. The structuralistic method is presented to us through a series of important characteristics, which aim at the main aspects, such as the way culture is seen. This was considered as having a systemic attribute and was considered as having to be analyzed as a complex and complete social form in which the necessary elements are combined in order to stimulate creativity and action, but in a close environment in which societies and groups of a certain culture are individually considered towards other societies. Analysts tributary to structuralism were considered researchers and observers detached of the analyzed object, and their investigations aiming society were directed towards the implied mechanisms, not towards the social actors or individuals. Thus there comes the active role of the reader in determining the meaning of a research, the relation between the reader and the written text being important, having multiple meanings, and the simple research of some formal structures not being sufficient.

Before talking about poststructuralism, first of all we have to remember that most of the methodologies used in social post-modern studies are bor-

---

[106] Wilson 2003, p.16.
[107] Glassie 2000, p. 18. Quote "When the builder's attention is narrowed by training, whether in the dusty shop of a master carpenter or the sleek classroom of a university, past experience is not obliterated. It endures in the strange caves of the brain and in the old habits of the muscles as they seek smooth routes through the air. Education adds a layer. In precept and admonition, in pedagogical technique, if not in content, the teacher brings cultural values into the process of transmission".
[108] Muredoch 2006, pp.4-11.

rowed from post-structuralism. Without structuralism, whose theories considered culture as being independent of the immediate meaning of existence, post-structuralism considered culture as an inseparable attribute of existence. Thus, structuralists were studying structures, which were at the base of the cultural product, such as the landscape and the text, and were using analytic concepts from linguistics, psychology and anthropology. Poststructuralism is difficult to define, as it denies the definitions from the past. The only meaning of any studied object is unconceivable such as unique existence, using varied theories and perspectives, which lead to mostly conflict interpretations. Thus, any communication way of value, even through the language of cultural landscape, carries a certain ambiguity, which makes its precise interpretation practically impossible.

It is obvious that cultural landscape can be understood as a cultural concept, which implies dealing with various types of analyses and studies in order to be interpreted and understood, being a code of knowledge.

Poststructuralism appeared in philosophy at the beginning of the 1960's and the most important names are Derrida, Deleuze, Foucault, Lyotard or Kristeva. At the same time this movement has its roots deeply developed in a (philosophical) older history, mentioning the influences of the phenomenology of Husserl, the hermeneutics of Heidegger, the psychoanalysis of Freud or the transcendental philosophy of Kant.

Poststructuralism brings new methods of analysis, investigation and understanding the surrounding world and the human existence. Thus, James Williams[109] makes a profound description of the main critics towards postrstructuralism, affirming that

> in poststructuralism, life is not to be defined solely by science, but by the layers of history and future creations captured in wider senses of language, thought and experience.[110]

We can take as an important aspect the way in which the new world economic order and the bases of the capitalist consumption society as well as the industrial and informational revolution influenced the evolution of thinking and of the human culture. Thus, a turning point was the beginning of the 60's in the 20th century, and the cultural moment that followed at the beginning of the 80's produced changes in the way to perceive and study the landscape, and cultural geography as a science managed to surpass the doctrines of the American school whose father was Sauer and to adopt new theories in the

---

[109] Williams 2005, pp. 15-17.
[110] Williams 2005, p. 16.

study of the cultural landscape. The theorists of cultural studies were the supporters of structuralists' and post-structuralists' theories, the French school having the greatest influence. We could consider the period between the 60's and the 80's of the 20th century as a defining stage in the coagulation and formation of several fundamental concepts and theories, which characterized the continental thinking.

Thus, the new cultural geography studies the processes and cultural meanings of the individual's life[111] and the community at different spatial levels, involving except geographers also specialists in different fields like culture theorists, anthropologists, sociologists, architects and town planners.

The theorists of the cultural geography is based on a much more complex concept of cultural landscape, such as a culture ensemble, which form the real whose history we have to perceive and understand in relation with the surrounding material reality. A reality, which together with the changes brought by postmodernism is associated to new parameters, which as Frederic Jameson says, led to the disappearance of the individual as entity and the apparition of community, this new entity to which the urban life is related. Jameson affirms that this meant "death of the subject"[112] or the disappearance of individualism.

At urban and social level having a speech on cultural landscape means having a speech on community, and the demographic growth and the transformations the towns have suffered like their expansion and the economic and social context led to cultural contradictions. Consequently, a series of new concepts and theories have been developed, and from the methodological point of view the analysis and understanding of the cultural landscape integrated aspects of religion, politic, material and immaterial culture, everything as a negation and critic towards the American cultural geography school initiated in Berkeley by Sauer and towards the interpretations later tackled by Jackson.

The discursive studies are in relation with poststructuralism, the ideologies being directly inscriptioned in language through the narrative structure of the speech, which influences the way the individual perceives the surrounding

---

[111] Bell 1978, p. 49. Quote "The individual was considered unique, with singular aspirations, and life assumed a greater sanctity and preciousness. The enhancement of the single life became a value for its own sake".

[112] Jameson 1998, p. 5.Quote "But now we need to introduce a new piece into this puzzle, which may help to explain why classical modernism is a thing of the past and why postmodernism should have taken its place. This new component is what is generally called the 'death of the subject' or, to say it in more conventional language, the end of individualism as such".

objects being in relation with different theories of power. The concepts of these types of a speech can be found in the works of Michel Foucault and Jugern Habermas, which are opposed to the Marxist type of ideological definition of the speech. Thus, the discourse type of Foucault must be seen both as a singular and a general one. In the acceptance of the general meaning the speech is not only built of words but also of architectural devices understood as heterogeneous ensembles which include institutions, buildings (architectural designs), what we call today urban landscape, legislative system, philosophic speeches and argumentations. Thus, architectural devices can be spatial units or groups of buildings, dwelling units, spaces and places with cultural connotations, which finally form the cultural landscape. The discursive landscape is the one that produces a certain way of communication, a language in which the power realities are converted in urban texts (polymorph).

Situational knowledge developed as a result of the studies by researchers in the 80's of the 20th century, in the cultural moment produced in sociology, anthropology, geography ad cultural sciences[113]. Iain Cook argues the relation between text and object of study in order to explain the importance of situational knowledge and used terms. Thus, he affirms the fact according to which the academic knowledge is situated ad the implicated actor, the researcher is always positioned[114]. Then he explains that this very state of facts, this known existence, which is clearly positioned in an active reality is the one which leads to understanding the processed and decoding the object of study, which can be at the same time a text, a language as the one noted on the landscape, in the built environment and their transformation into texts.

Briefly we can affirm that everywhere around us there is knowledge. It exists in different coded and most of the times hidden ways, which wait to be deciphered. Thus the situational knowledge is specific of a certain situation, through which the spectator owns a certain piece of information, and which he uses for a certain purpose. Subjectivity, which is closely connected with people's experience and the way to learn, leads to an advanced situational

---

[113] Cook 2005, p. 16. Quote "The main point they make is that academic and other knowledges are always situated, always produced by positioned actors working in/between all kinds of locations, working up/on/through all kinds of research relations(hips)".

[114] Cook 2005, p. 16. Quote "thus, so the argument goes, writing about academic knowledge as a relational process rather than a straightforward thing might highlight the politics of knowledge in academic research, produce more modest, embodied, partial, locatable and convincing arguments and, in the process, make it possible for researchers (and their audience) to see and make all kinds of, often unexpected, politically progressive connections".

knowledge, which has its bases in culture and traditions and language as well.

In building our argumentation we need to mention that knowledge based on experience is called a posteriori, but there is also a priori knowledge which Immanuel Kant considered transcendental knowledge and the a posteriori one empiric[115]. Types of a priori knowledge are extremely rare, but between these there is time and space. A posteriori knowledge appeals to the researcher's identity and practices, which build his experience, but which does not offer any guarantee of complete deciphering of the hidden code of the object of study, thus the meaning being partial, and knowledge being incomplete, the individual having to know the studied object through a limited number of pieces of information.

In his trial to put culture in the center of geography's study as a science, Carl Ortwin Sauer published in 1925 the well-known essay entitled *The Morphology of Landscape*, as a critique towards environmental determinism. In this work he characterized the cultural landscape as

> fashioned from the natural landscape by a culture group. Culture is the agent the natural area is the medium, the cultural landscape the result.[116]

Nevertheless, the last aspect of his morphological study on landscape was regarding the human individual, which he sees as the

> most important morphologic factor.[117]

Thinking about the morphology of landscape, we might want to add something regarding the contemporary urban landscapes, because much has changed since Sauer's thesis on morphology. In this particular paper he wrote about the concept of cultural landscape, thus being one of the forerunners of cultural geography and cultural landscape studies. Although this is one of the first writings on cultural landscape in American studies in geography, on the other part of the Atlantic ocean, German geographers were also interested into the cultural landscape studies, but with a slightly different approach. In Germany, geography began to exist as a scientific discipline during the 1880's, and the major field of study was human geography and the concern

---

[115] Kant 2004, p. 27. Quote "The possibility of synthetic propositions a posteriori, i.e., of such as are drawn from experience, also requires no special explanation; for experience itself is nothing other than a continual conjoining (synthesis) of perceptions. There remain for us therefore only synthetic propositions a priori, whose possibility must be sought or investigated, since it must rest on principles other than the principle of contradiction".
[116] Sauer 1963, p. 343.
[117] Sauer 1963, p. 341.

was mostly on urban areas and their existence. Therefore, the most known names in this field were Friedrich Ratzel and Walter Geisler[118], they being interested in the study of place, location and genetic question regarding the existence of large cities. Geisler was recalled by Sauer in his essay, as an example of great contribution to the field of cultural form studies.[119] As Sauer stated,

> the cultural landscape is the geographic area in the final meaning[120]

and we could argue that the cultural landscape, in it's most pure way is the urban landscape (or rural and small town landscape at a different scale than the large city and town areas). Referring to Sauer's thesis, Mitchell said:

> Sauer's main purpose was to show that the environmental determinism had pretty much got it backwards. It wasn't nature that caused culture, but rather culture, working with and on nature, created the contexts of life. Sauer was especially concerned with material aspects of culture, particularly the landscape, which he saw as manifestations of culture's traffic with nature.[121]

Thus we can affirm that Sauer based his argument on the thesis according to which the proof of cultural variety was the landscape, which was considered a manifestation of the culture, that produced it.

The above mentioned essay is the climax of Sauer's theory, in which the methodological aspects are presented. In what he called a

> diagrammatic representation of the morphology of the cultural landscape[122]

he gave a definition of the concept as regards geography:

> Its forms are all the works of man that characterise the landscape. Under this definition we are not concerned in geography with the energy, customs, or beliefs of man but with man's record upon the landscape. Forms of population are the phenomena of mass or density in general and of recurrent displacement, as seasonal migration. Housing includes the types of structures man builds and their grouping, either dispersed as in many rural districts, or agglomerated into villages or cities in varying plans. Form of production are the types of land util-

---

[118] Walter Geisler published his original book entitled *Die deutsche Stadt: ein Beitrag zur Morphologie der Kulturlandschaft* in 1924 in *Forschungen zur deutschen Landes- und Volkskunde (Engelhorn, Stuttgart).*

[119] Sauer 1963, p. 342. Sauer wrote: „Most recently, Walter Geisler has undertaken a synthesis of the urban forms of Germany, with the deserved subtitle, <<A contribution to the morphology of the cultural landscape>>".

[120] Sauer 1963, p. 342.

[121] Mitchell 2000, p. 21.

[122] Sauer 1963, p. 342. The subchapter in his work called *Diagrammatic representation of the morphology of the cultural landscape* is where he gives the definition of the concept of cultural landscape.

ization for primary products, farms, forests, mines, and those negative areas which he has ignored.[123]

What is very important is for us to understand the culture's theories, which led to the understanding the Sauer gave to the cultural landscape and to the importance it had in cultural geography. Mitchell was the one that made a short incursion in the theories that influenced Sauer and resumed in his work:

> Far less clear is what, for Sauer, actually constitutes ,<<culture>> beyond some vague sense of historically, geographically derived <<difference>>. Culture seems to him a <<hole>>, simply an unproblematic <<way of life>> of a people. (…) It is <<culture>> that determines social life, for Sauer, but the exact nature of that culture remains a mystery.[124]

The well known geographer is not interested in studying customs or beliefs of different cultural groups. Thus, by studying landforms and landscape morphology, Sauer rapidly came to realize the importance of the human cultures to the landscape transformations, as one of the key aspects of morphology studies in geography. Therefore, at the end of his well known work, Sauer concluded that

> Altogether we deal with the interrelation of group, or cultures, and site, as expressed in the various landscapes of the world.[125]

Like Carl Sauer, John Brinckerhoff Jackson played a remarkable and accelerating role in the study of the cultural landscape in the United States.

In most of his essays, he was trying to explain the meaning of the word landscape[126] and how it should be understood as

---

[123] Sauer 1963, pp. 342-343.
[124] Mitchell 2000, p. 24.
[125] Sauer 1963, p. 349. For a more complete understanding of his words, the full paragraph must be cited here: „In the colorful reality of life there is a continuous resistance of fact to confinement within any <<simpliste>> theory. We are concerned with <<directed activity, not premature realization>>, and this is the morphologic approach. Our naively selected section of reality, the landscape, is undergoing manifold change. This contact of man with his changeful home, as expressed through the cultural landscape, is our field of work. We are concerned with the importance of the site to man, and also with his transformation of the site. Althougether we deal with the interrelation of group, or cultures, and site, as expressed in the various landscapes of the world. Here are an inexhaustible body of fact and variety of relations which provide a course of inquiry that does not need to restrict itself to the straits of rationalism".
[126] Jackson 1984, p. 6. We believe that a very important quote must be noted here, from Jackson's work: „This is very confusing, and even more confusing is the fact that to this day in Scotland a *land* means a building divided into houses or flats. I confess that I find this particular use of the word hard to decipher, except that in Gaelic the word *lann* means an enclosed space. Finally, here is an example – if it can be called that – of *land* meaning bouth a fraction of a larger space and an enclosed space".

a space on the surface of the earth.[127]

But we should not take this at the very simplistic way, as this meaning is much more complex as Jackson itself tried to explain. He even argues that the word landscape has won his freedom, as we all use it in a variety of ways, explaining things that are not related to geography or the environment. Here we can refer to different ways of using it, like landscape of meaning, landscape of thoughts, landscape of dreams, landscape of power, political landscape or the landscape of poetry or many others that I can't think of right now. Extrapolating this, we could come to the meaning of the words cityscape, townscape, roadscape, as Jackson said that the word scape means space; a space of the city, a space of the town or a space of the land.

> Yet they remind us of an important truth: that we always need a word or phrase to indicate a kind of environment or setting which can give vividness to a thought or event or relationship; a background placing it in the world.[128]

In Jackson's works we discover the relation between the words landscape and community and their meanings. Therefore we find out that the landscape is made by the community for the community. In a more understandable and simplified manner, the landscape is not natural, it is a man made synthetic organization of forms. This being said, we must bear in mind that a natural landscape still exists, and it was the background for the human intervention on the land forms in order for the human existence to evolve and for the communities to grow.[129]

After gaining a vast experience in the study of the cultural landscape, Jackson wrote in the first issue of the *Landscape* magazine in 1951:

> Wherever we go, whatever the nature of our work, we adorn the face of the earth with a living design which changes and is eventually replaces by that of the future generation. (…) The city is an essential part of this shifting and growing design, but only a part of it. Beyond the last street light, out where the familiar asphalt ends, a whole country waits to be discovered: villages, farmsteads and highways, half-hidden valleys of irrigated gardens, and wide land-

---

[127] Jackson 1984, p. 5.
[128] Jackson 1984, p. 4.
[129] Jackson 1984, pp. 7-8. John Brinckerhoff Jackson said: „Nevertheless the formula *landscape as a composition of man-made spaces on the land* is more significant than it first appears, for if it does not provide us with a definition it throws a revealing light on the origin of the concept. For it says that a landscape is not a natural feature of the environment but a *synthetic* space, a man made system of spaces superimposed on the face of the land, functioning and evolving not according to natural laws but to serve a community – for the collective character of the landscape is one thing that all generations and all points of view have agreed upon".

scapes reaching to the horizon. A rich and beautiful book is always open before us. We have but to learn to read it.[130]

Jackson was constantly interested in the study of the landscape. From the beginning of his career as a publicist he was preoccupied by the cultural landscape and the adaptation of the theories and concepts on architecture, urbanism and landscape architecture, mainly as reactions and personal critics on modernism. Wilson said in his book about Jackson:

> The potential role of designers in making a more meaningful environment was a consistent theme in his writing, and he was vitally interested in the cultural and social meaning of architectural design.[131]

In 1934 he came to Europe, where he had the opportunity to observe and study the constructions of the modern avant-garde architecture: Le Corbusier, Mies van der Rohe or Walter Gropius, whom he called:

> ridiculous, intellectual architecture.[132]

Mainly his works, which criticized modern architecture and the International Style, were written under the pseudonym H.G. West, Jackson having the capacity to write very differently according to the pseudonym he chose due to the literature studies he had and his vast editorial experience. Thus, from Jackson's (West) affirmations the conclusion is that modernism (as regarding architecture) would be the supporter of the dogma

> that the architect knows better than the client.[133]

He was fascinated by vernacular American landscape, that was in the centre of many of his writings. But the evolution of technology and the rapid change in mobility and transport were the issues for his most important themes: cars, roads and mobility. As he stated,

> in Europe every city has individuality, whereas in our country it is often hard to distinguish one city from another. With the possible exception of Boston and New Orleans and San Francisco, they not only are lacking in architectural variety, they are lacking in landmarks and in unique neighbourhoods. (...) Most of us (...) would say that a sense of place, a sense of being at home in a town or city, grows as we become accustomed to it and learn to know its peculiarities. It is my own belief that a sense of place is something that we ourselves create in the course of time. (...) But others disagree. They believe that a sense of place comes from our response to features which are already there – either a beautiful natural

---

[130] Wilson 2003. p. 9.
[131] Wilson 2003, p. 13.
[132] Wilson 2003, p. 41.
[133] Wilson 2003, p. 43.

setting or well-designed architecture. They believe that a sense of place comes from being in an unusual composition of spaces and forms.[134]

His argument is very important for what the cultural townscape is in the modern city, and his view we consider is partly correct, just that in our belief, the two opinions are to be correlated in order to make the sense of a place. Let us just think about the places we lived in as a child, our hometown, the backyard or the grandparents house.

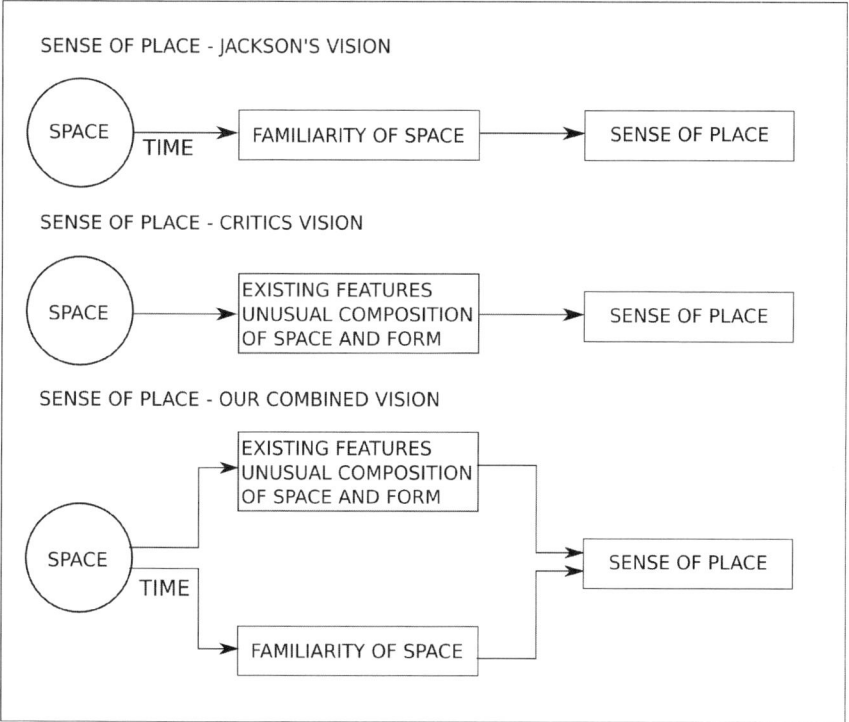

Illustration 1: Jackson's vision on space. Graphic by the author.

Those are spaces that make sense of place as regards our own vision of that space, and in particular they are special landmarks, even icons of our own lives, that are important for us and remain in our memories forever, as Andrew Ballantyne argued:

---

[134] Jackson 1994, p. 151.

One of the things that make our surroundings feel right is familiarity. We grow accustomed to our surroundings and shape our habits around them, so that even if the surroundings interfere with what we're trying to do, we are accustomed to dealing with the problems. Buildings which are part of the daily scene come to have significance simply by being there.[135]

In contrast to this argument, Jackson takes a different approach on the public space:

> every traditional public space, whether religious or political or ethnic in character, displays a variety of symbols, inscriptions, images, monuments, not as works of art but to remind people of their civic privileges and duties.[136]

This is how he sees the public space, which, in our opinion, still has the potential to make the sense of place, not only the private one. Lets add to our list from above (the one with the backyard and the grandparents house), the center of our hometown, or the small square in the neighbourhood. Those too, are places, not just spaces. Places for the ones that spend time there, not just for the ones that live in a space. The sense of place is given by us through the visions we have on the surrounding reality, and by the icons and symbols that the transformed landscape gives us as a preexisting datum.

Another great mind and with great influence in cultural geography was Yi-Fu Tuan, whose most known work, *Space and Place* had a significant impact on the study of awareness of place. He was also interested on the urban aspects of life and how architectural space can change or make sense of place for the urban citizen.

> How does modern architectural space affect awareness? In important respects, the principal ways by which it influences people and society have not changed. Architectural space continues to articulate the social order, though perhaps with less blatancy and rigidity than it did in the past. The modern built environment even maintains a teaching function: its signs and posters inform and expostulate. Architecture continues to exert a direct impact on the senses and feeling. (...) Architects, with the help of technology, continue to enlarge the range of human spatial consciousness by creating new forms or by remaking old ones.[137]

Furthermore he uses the following definition of place:

> place is whatever stable object catches our attention[138],

saying that where-ever we look, our eye tends to search for a landmark, a special something that will make our sight to pause in order to find/give the

---
[135] Ballantyne 2002, p. 32.
[136] Jackson 1984, p. 18.
[137] Tuan 2008, p. 116.
[138] Tuan 2008, p. 161.

sense of a certain place. This has a particular aspect in the urban landscape, where everywhere you look there are symbols, icons and signs that make the character of a place and give the individual the sense of awareness. Outside the city, in the modern world, everything has evolved, and almost everywhere you can find a sign of a certain type, whether you are on the highway, on a country road, in a forest or up in the mountains.

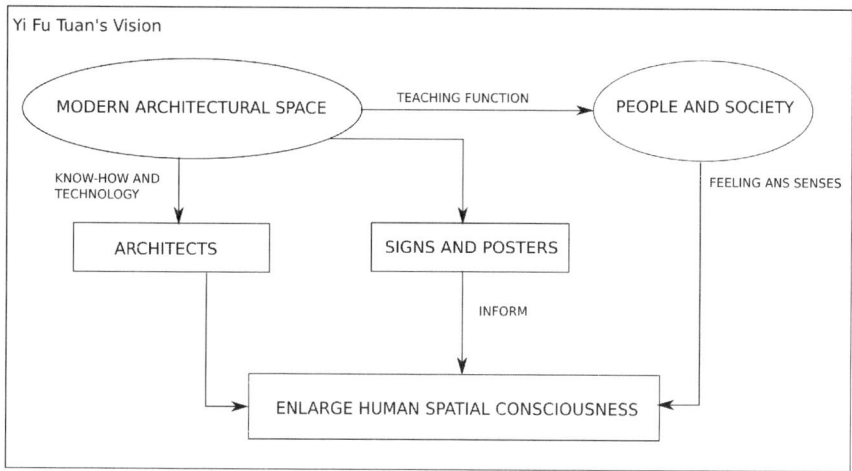

Illustration 2: Yi-Fu Tuan's vision on modern urban space and awareness. Graphic by the author.

The cultural moment from the beginning of the 80's produced changes in the way to perceive and study the landscape, and cultural geography as a science managed to surpass the doctrines of the American school, whose father was Sauer, and to adopt new theories in the study of cultural landscape. The new cultural geography carries on the study of the cultural processes and significations of the individual's life, at different special levels, implying besides geographers specialists from several branches, as well as theorists of culture, anthropologists, sociologists, and last but not least town planers. Thus, the theorists of the new cultural geography ground on a much more complex landscape concept, as a culture ensemble, which form the real, whose history we have to perceive and understand in relation to the surrounding material reality. As a consequence a series of new concepts and theories were developed, and from the methodological point of view the analysis and understanding the cultural landscape integrated aspects related to religion, politics, material and immaterial culture as a negation and critique towards the American school of cultural geography initiated at Berkeley by Sauer and towards the interpretations approached later by Jackson.

Even though it has very few to deal with the geographical vision, it is worth talking about Deleuze's and Guattari's vision about the landscape and the city environment. What was important to this study was the book of Andrew Ballantyne called *Deleuze and Guattari for Architects*, in which some very interesting ideas and arguments are raised.

> Opening up to the outside, where things are different from the territory we know and inhabit, has its dangers. If we make it a constant habit then we might find that we have lost any sense of who we are, and have become schizophrenic.[139]

This is how chapter four of Ballantyne's book starts. It is indeed a way of living and dealing with the real that is schizophrenic. It is the way of the contemporary individual to get to understand and to accept the surrounding realities, where

> he does not live nature as nature, but as process of production. There is no such thing as either man or nature now, only a process that produces the one within the other and couples the machines together.[140]

This is how the two thinkers correlate the vision of the surrounding reality with the way a schizophrenic mind is seeing, as we sometimes tend to project the image of oneself into the landscape thinking that the sense of the world is how we see ourselves reflected in it.[141]

The vision of the landscape as a face and the similarities between the functions of the face and the landscape was important in the work of the two thinkers in the second volume of *Capitalism and Schizophrenia, A Thousand Plateaus* where they state that

> face and landscape manuals formed a pedagogy, a strict discipline, and were an inspiration to the arts as much as the arts were an inspiration to them. Architecture position its ensembles – houses, towns and cities, monuments or factories – to function like faces in the landscape they transform. (...) All faces envelop an unknown, unexplored landscape.[142]

The association of face and landscape also appears in the works of Anne Buttimer who stated that

---

[139] Ballantyne 2007, p. 61.
[140] Deleuze, Guattari 1972 cited Ballantyne 2007, p. 63.
[141] Ballantyne 2007.
[142] Deleuze, Guattari 1980 cited Ballantyne 2007, p. 67.

geographical language is thoroughly metaphorical. The sur-'face' of the earth has been described in terms of eyes, nose, mouth, cheek, and profile; it has been named and claimed with terms derived from human anatomy and society. Regions and hamlets have been likened to organisms; roadways and canals, to arteries of circulation. Industrial complexes have been described in terms of mechanical processes steered by growth poles as generators of economic development.[143]

Illustration 3: Graffiti drawing in Vienna. Territorial marker as a face. A metaphorical view on landscape as face. Image by the author.

Buttimer also refers to place names which

> whether real or imaginary, such El Dorado, Mecca, Waterloo, and Eden, symbolize particular kinds of experience. Colonists and new settlers often blithely change place names as a mark of occupance. Geographers have labeled places and territories with the metaphor of science.[144]

Talking about language and place names we must refer to the works of prof. Peter Jordan, whose writings on cultural landscape and geographical names were of much interest for my research. He states that place names shapes the cultural landscape in two distinct ways:

---

[143] Buttimer 1993, p. 77.
[144] Buttimer 1993, p. 77.

visibly (visible in the landscape) in signposts in front of settlements, at administrative boundaries like communal or provincial borders or at state borders, also along roads and highways and in streets. But place names shape geographical space also mentally by labelling spatial concepts (space-related ideas and images). In this way they support structuring geographical space, since name and concept are mostly closely linked.[145]

The matter of place names is a very complex and interesting domain, with direct implications in the cultural landscape evolution.

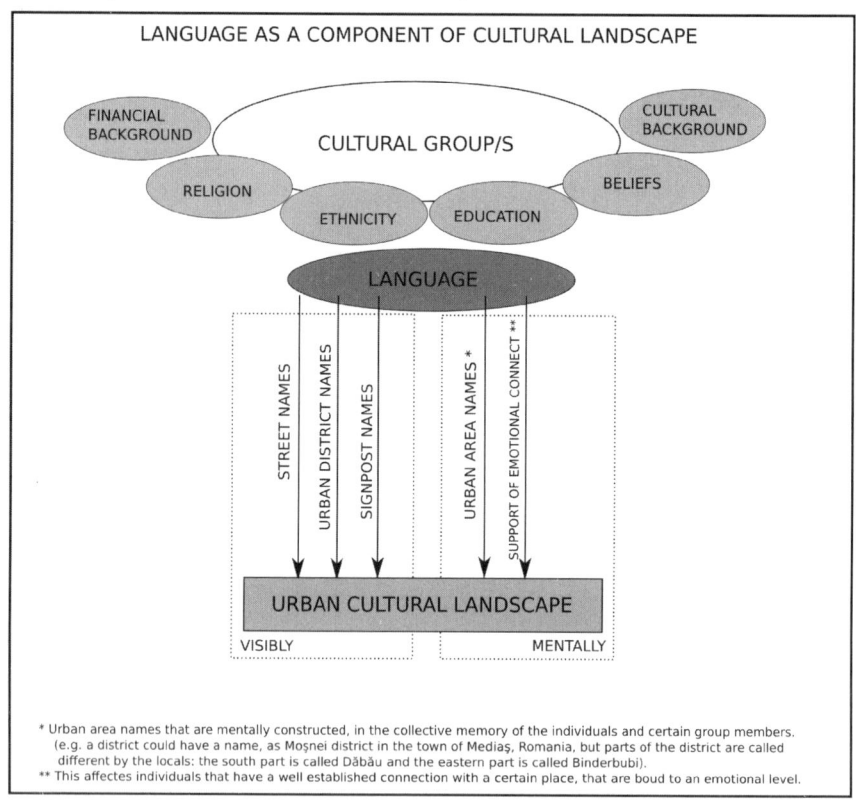

Illustration 4: Language as a component of cultural landscape. Peter Jordan's vision on language and place names. Graphic by the author.

---

[145] Jordan 2009, p. 36.

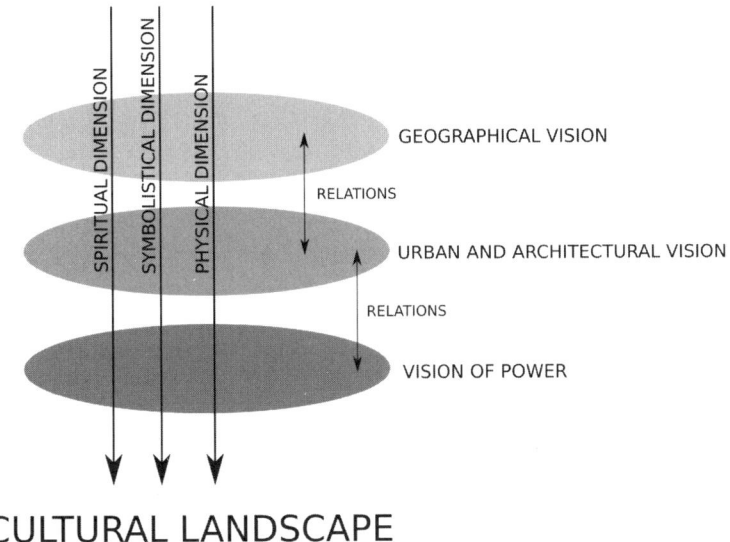

Illustration 5: Sketch on the idea of visions. A layer structure of the cultural landscape as a palimpsest. Graphic by the author.

Therefore, while talking about cultural landscapes, even urban ones, we can't escape the matter of place names. Urban areas, dominated by specific groups (e. g. ethnic minorities) have names that have the roots in the cultural background of that social group. Even names of the cities, towns or villages are sometimes influenced and dictated by the cultural background of the dominating social group or inspired by the customs or in extremis by religious matters. Certain areas within the city have distinct names depending on the cultural group that live there. Street names are part of the cultural group and even different dialects of the multitude of languages that are used within a city are important aspects of the cultural landscape. Talking about the urban cultures is in direct connection with language patterns, dialects and street signs. In extremis, we can refer to graffiti drawings in the city, that are territorial markers, mostly used by groups with a specific cultural belonging (e.g. gang members influenced by a certain type of culture or sub-culture).

Illustration 6: Image by the author of an Oil Painting courtesy of Amelia Prostean. Reproduction with prior consent of the artist.

Architectural and urban visions

The city is not just a material construction. It has a mental construct component that makes it an imagined space. First of all, the city is the reflection of ideas of urban designers, planners and architects, and how they thought it (the city) should look, work and feel. It is the mental construct of individuals belonging to (at least it should be) an elite group of the society. Therefore the city represents the materialization of the power of ideas, visions and imaginations, being a support layer for the different layers of tensions and relations.

The city is a space imagined and one of imagination, the one of the collective and the individual. As Aart Mekking points out,

> architecture and urbanism are expressions of non-material phenomena. (...) This explains why new things-to-be-built are always and everywhere, to a certain extent, based on a selection from already existing building traditions.[146]

That is why we talk about a representation of the reality, a mental construct, about the visions of what seems to be the paradigm of architectural representation[147]: the real. Thus, subjectivity always played a major role in reading and decoding the surrounding reality.

What is real and how do we know if our opinion about the real is true is a question that had preoccupied researchers from the beginning. In order to be able to verify the scientific argumentation generally it is necessary to have a series of empiric data based on the observation and investigation of the outer environment. The simple relation object - text is replaced by a more complex one in which both the researcher and the audience are given a role in the process of decoding a language, the text of the urban landscape, mentioning the notion which Derrida assigns to reading:

> Our ability to understand relies on our capacity to interpret signs. It also presupposes that signs come to signify in ways that no particular author or speaker can constrain in advance trough intention.[148]

This is similar to what David Frisby states in his book *Cityscapes of Modernity* when he talks about the mysteries of the city

> that presupposes a notion of reading the city as text.[149]

The city was always a mystery, a place of apparent chaos with a vast diversity of experiences, and it was a real puzzle for its reader. The individual's reading of the city is in a metaphoric way somehow a detective fiction reading, in which the city is a ordered and controlled text. This text is the body of the mental construct that is the real and it reveals itself as something exclusive and unique, a series of stimulations and interests of the modern life in the city, a cultural dynamic discourse of symbols. Thus, the contemporary city bears history, being characterized by major transformations at the level of all elements, which build the urban structure and the social life, thus no experience being singular. Everything is related to vicinity, to the elements, which

---

[146] Mekking 2009, p. 23.
[147] Mekking 2009.
[148] Murdoch 2006, p. 8.
[149] Frisby 2007, p. 53.

determine it and to the memory of the past experiences. Sharon Zukin stated how cities were often criticised due to the fact that

> they represent the basest instincts of human society[150]

and Hannah Arendt that

> the clear sign that society represents the public organization of the very process of life is maybe the fact that in a relatively short time the new social domain transformed all modern communities in societies of workers and employees.[151]

As Deleuze and Guattari described the forces that are necessary to make a town live, they stated that a town is always part of a *milieu* and is connected to a network that is part of the environment:

> If I am in the town, then it is my environment, but the town itself is between other towns, which make its environment. Any 'thing' can be described as an environment if we think of it at an appropriate scale[152]

and

> at another scale: if I am in search of an intensification of humans, then I head for the city.[153]

This is, in other words, a perfect description of the city as a metropolis, as Georg Simmel wrote in 1903:

> the metropolitan type (...) creates a protective organ for itself against the profound disruption with which the fluctuations and discontinuities of the external milieu threaten it.[154]

Similar to the visions we are trying to discuss about in this paper, Max Weber had an approach on the different concepts of the city in 1921. But, in none of those described by him, the cultural concept or category of the city was to be put in discussion, while he talks about the economical concept, the consumer, producer and merchant city, about the economic development, socio political concept.[155] But is not to be forgotten that there is significant importance of the cultural theory and history in the evolution of cities. For this, philosophy and thought played a major role as Dewey argued. He wrote about the connection of philosophy and culture and the civilization and the way that culture was changed by philosophy:

---

[150] Zukin 2000, p. 132.
[151] Arendt 2007, p. 43.
[152] Ballantyne 2007, p. 81.
[153] Ballantyne 2007, p. 80.
[154] Simmel 2008, p. 97.
[155] Weber 2008.

> Philosophy thus sustains the closest connection with the history of culture, with the succession of changes in civilization. It is fed by the streams of tradition, traced at critical moments to their sources in order that the current may receive a new direction; it is fertilized by the ferment of new inventions in industry, new explorations of the globe, new discoveries in science.[156]

The contemporary city is a result of all the actions and thoughts that shaped the way people saw the urban life, in order to give their existence a meaning and as Lewis Mumford stated,

> we must now conceive the city, accordingly, not primarily as a place of business or government, but as an essential organ for expressing and actualizing the new human personality.[157]

Thus, in the sphere of the modern (and post-modern), the architect represents the world of certainty and power by the unification and rationalisation of space. Here, both time and space have other coordinates, the city being just a fragment of reality. The everyday of contemporary life thus proves that a metaphysic city or a pure architectural philosophical system is a utopia by its work, the architect proposing a complex experience, which reunites time, space, tradition, creativity and the senses. The sensitivity of space is given to us by the senses with which we perceive it, by the way in which we observe the configuration and the way we realize it. Space is, as we have mentioned before, a system of relations, a space of feeling, in which every thing finds its place, that is the normality to exist, and the understanding of the cultural landscape is strictly connected to this normality of existence and space which

> juxtaposes or overlaps the <<tracks>> of several former periods, whose original significations escapes us, because every track is reinterpreted and reintegrated in the contemporary functional context.[158]

We can also mention Lefebvre, who considered that in the actual space both past and future rule, being loaded with significations of the social life. Thus a return of the sensitiveness must be taken into consideration, a new beginning in the configuration of the social, a solution to the passivity and lack of cohesion of the individual in the social life, through the emphasis on formations and relations, which could help at the affirmation of the difference between the subjects. Iain S. Black used at the beginning of his work *(Re)reading architectural landscapes* Olsen's following quotation from 1986:

---

[156] Dewey 2008, p. 112.
[157] Mumford 2008, p. 131.
[158] Mihali, Copoeru 2002, p. 11.

> What messages were buildings, cities, and other works of art expected to transmit? What meaning did they possess, what ideas did they contain? What can a city, in its capacity as a work of art, accomplish? What can art do, apart from existing in its own right? It can tell a story, or many stories. It can establish a mood. It can reinforce selected virtues, textures, colours and movements. It can stand for, or represent, ideas, qualities, institutions.[159]

Here the character of cultural product of the city is very well underlined, as well as the character of cultural process of the city, in which difference is the engine of social life of the individual, what feeds the dynamic of the urban landscape. We are given a new dimension of the urban experience, the city offering at the same time a public space of culture and a more familiar one, the private space of culture. Thus,

> cities reflect a great fear of exposure, and are constructed instead to protect our inner (even spiritual) selves from the threat of social contact and from differences.[160]

We shall not make here the confusion between urban cultural landscape and urban image. We consider the two components to be different, even if up to a point they seem to have a similar meaning. In order to know and interpret the urban cultural landscape we need much more than the direct observation of a frame, or a image.

The role of the observer is complex and in order to interpret the symbols we need a solid training prior to the observation. In this context we need to remind what John Leighly said in his volume entitled *Land and Life. A selection from the writings of Carl Ortwin Sauer*[161] regarding the attention, which Sauer gave in the first years of his research to the way in which the human settlements were created (mainly in the studies of cultural areas) as a very important aspect in the study and understanding the cultural landscape. Maybe because of this the term was lavishly used in contexts which lead to confusion and misunderstanding.

---

[159] Black 2003, p. 19.
[160] Bridge, Watson 2000, p. 10.
[161] Sauer 1963, p. 5. John Leighly in the introduction of the volume entitled *Land and Life. A selection from the writings of Carl Ortwin Sauer*: "The shaping of the cultural landscape is a cumulative process, each stage of which conditions the next one; the first stage is therefore the most critical one".

Illustration 7: The view of a house through a water-soap baloon. A metaphor of seeing the city: is not just an image, is a representation that needs to be interpreted, decoded and understood. Is a complex of symbols and signs that lets you see only a snapshot of the real (e.g. in the photo the house) but in the same time warns you about the multitude of interpretations (e.g. in the photo there are two different views of the same house in only one baloon, from one point of observation – the photographer's position). Image by the author.

The cultural landscape has always been and will always be a mediator between the past and the future, a metaphor which expresses the memories, the needs and the social experiences. The urban landscape is a representation through which the buildings, objects, spaces, individuals are correlated with events by the mental concepts and representations, which every one of us produce and use in a complex system of relations in everyday life. Thus culture became a desideratum in every process of knowing the space, urbanity or landscape. It is a representation system, through which everything that means urban life is substituted to a set of symbols, associations and relations, which lead to understanding the spaces through a complex system of concepts.

The contemporary urban landscape is a space where identities are formed, being active and dynamic. Understanding it is a complex phenomenon, being both a cultural process and a cultural product. The process of social life is directly integrated in the notion of urban landscape, Eric Hirsch stating that the landscape

> is a cultural process that brings together the cultural meaning of landscape with the concrete actuality of everyday life.[162]

The terminology of landscape next to the term urban is relatively new and implies knowing and understanding both. The way to read the landscape, being either natural, cultural or urban, is connected to both its immediate content, its visual, and its mental and sensitive content of individual or collective memory. In many writings the urban landscape is called also architectural landscape or townscape, implying one of the important characteristics of architecture, that the form is never neutral, it takes part to constructing the identity as a component of the cultural landscape by the mental aspect and the sensitivity which the space for living and social life adds. The trials to always find out what is not supposed to be seen with the naked eye led to discovering relations and causes, which are important in the control and transformation of the landscape, and they emphasized the fact that the landscape is still for the most part culturally determined. Pier Carlo Palermo states that

> the fragmented and sometimes chaotic image of many contemporary urban landscapes probably expresses the uncertain coexistence of a plurality of partial orders, still little understood[163]

with reference to the fragmented image of many contemporary cities as a result of the coexistence of different cultures and the relations between them. But, in the same time, the danger of losing the city exists, as Frampton states that

> the vulgarization of architecture and its progressive isolation from society have of late driven the discipline in upon itself, so that (...) this tendency reduces architectonic elements to pure syntactical signs that signify nothing outside their own 'structural' operation; at its most nostalgic it celebrates the loss of the city.[164]

Thus, while referring to the urban landscape we refer to relations. The dualism of these relations can be taken also from what Russell West-Pavlov said, referring to Lefebvre, who considered that space

---

[162] Hirsch 1995, p. 3.
[163] Palermo 2008, p. 32.
[164] Frampton 2007, p. 10.

is not a pre-existing container for artefacts and practices, but is constituted by them in a relationship of reciprocal influence and inflection.[165]

These relations, which define the urban landscape and the co-existence of different cultures in the urban space, are very well outlined by Theodor Adorno :

> if it were possible some kind of analysis of the typical culture of today, if the absolute dominance of the economic did not ridicule any trial to explain the actual surroundings by the spiritual life of its victims and if the very analyst hadn't sworn faith to this very situation, then such an investigation should prove that the fitting illness for our times is the very normality.[166]

Illustration 8: The Palace of Parliament, former People's House, in Bucharest, Romania, the second largest building in the World after the U.S. Pentagon. Image by the author.

Here is a normality which is differently perceived in every historic period. A normality, which is never the same for all the cities, not even for every individual. But we can admit that we are talking about a normality, which is shaped based on a multitude of cultures, which form the contemporary society. In this train of thoughts we can ask ourselves, what does the urban land-

---
[165] Pavlov 2009, p. 24.
[166] Adorno 2007, p. 70.

scape represent for the modern man, or, better, what does the landscape represent from the individual's perspective, which in essence is urban.

Therefore we can state that the cultural landscape has very much to do with the community and the pursuit of happiness in the modern city and for the modern man. We know that, since the beginning, the goal of the citizens was to achieve happiness in the environment they lived in, in our case the urban, and that

> people not only *can* be happy, but that they *should* be happy – that they are destined for happiness in this life and thereby have a natural right to it.[167]

The urban space and its architecture is shaping the citizens everyday life, thus urban form and planning are important aspects for the interpretation of the cultural urban landscapes. As the cities grow larger and larger, the pursuit of happiness became similar with the escape from the city, and the modern citizen is looking for happiness outside the core of the city, trying to escape the dangers and frustrations that the city life - cosmopolite life, brings.

Furthermore we would like to point out what Ian Black stated regarding the methods for architectural cultural landscape interpretation and how this should be multi-scale, sensitive to context and multi-criterial and multi-method. As he argues

> in short, to provide a fuller analysis of the forces behind the production of particular built environments, and to try to establish the way they were perceived and used, a range of methods and sources needs to be brought to bear upon the particular architectural landscape that caught the imagination in the first place.[168]

His argument is then supported with the statements regarding the use of multiple methods to highlight the consistencies and to

> identify inconsistencies that might throw new light on why particular architectural landscapes were built, where they were built, for whom, and how they were represented and used.[169]

In the socialist cities of Romania, quick urbanisation and industrialization ended in creating massive collective housing quarters and new public spaces as civic centres of the towns, with the influence of Le Corbusier's concepts in urbanism and architecture. Local adaptations on architecture[170] had an im-

---

[167] Bartetzky, Schalenberg 2009, p. 7.
[168] Black 2003, p. 27.
[169] Black 2003, p. 28.
[170] The Palace of Parliament in Bucharest is registered in the World Records Book as being on the second place, at Administrative buildings section, after the Pentagon, with its 330.000

mense impact on the different ways the urban space was created, for example differences between regions as the centre and the southern part of the country. The somehow integrated approach in architecture and urban planning from the beginning of the 20th century found its end at the start of the Second World War, and the state of confusion and complete denial of post-war interventions and architecture still persists. In the post-socialist city, the trial to surpass the local lyric functionalism of the communist period ended in adapting an architecture and urban planning that needs a much more integrated approach and a better understanding of the urban cultural landscape that is part of our life and our reality and has an history that needs to be accepted and from which we need to learn to create the future.

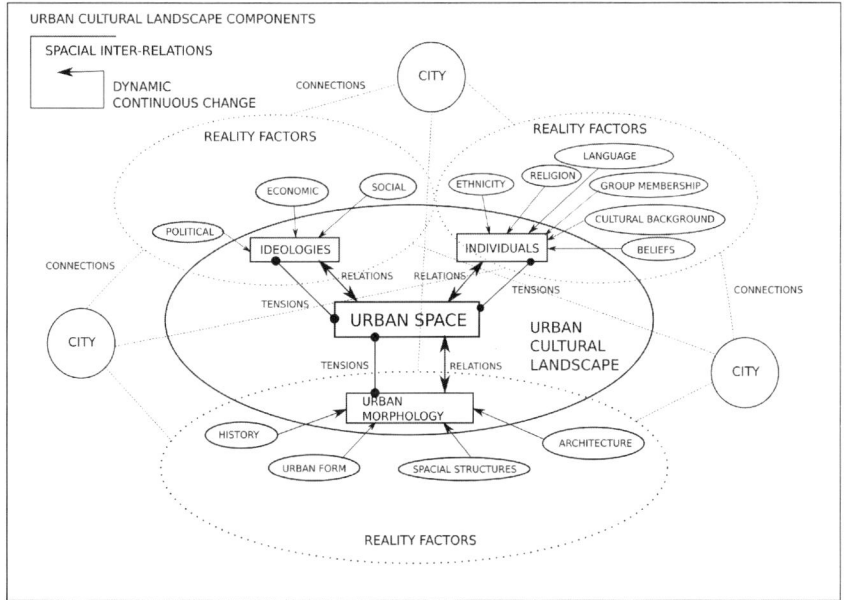

Illustration 9: The author's vision on cultural landscape, it's components and the connections between the existing cities that create a continuous dynamic change. Graphic by the author.

---

square meters area. It is on the 3rd place with regard to it's 2.550.000 cubic meters volume, just after the Cape Canaveral's rocket assembly building. This information has been adapted and translated by the author from the website www.casapoporului.ro accessed on 25th june 2010, 19.56 hrs.

THE CULTURAL LANDSCAPE AS A LANDSCAPE OF POWER

The moment that led to the migration of people from village to town was characterized by the industrial revolution, and materialized in the starting point of a society lead by a force of mass production, of social mobility and absolute contrasts. New technologies and ideas led to the transformation of inter-human relationships and to the re-thinking of the individual's position in the rapid change of the urban landscape. Thus the urban landscape forms what Robert Ezra Park called a "moral order"[171] or Sharon Zukin a "landscape of power"[172], of (dis)order and of progress.

Thus, in order to understand the progress and the becoming of the landscape through culture it is important to accept the opposability of two ways to interpret and observe the landscape, like Bourdieu, who had the central theme of his works the trial to surpass the paradox subjective / objective through the study of the relations between the material and symbolic dimensions of social life. Identity is the one that defines and emphasizes the difference, both regarding the individual and the landscape. In the study of the latter one, the notions of memory and place are essential in defining community. And memory and place through landscape are important decoding instruments of the symbols at different levels, from local to regional and global.

The urban cultural landscape is like a theatrical stage, a frame full of symbols in which the parade of power takes place, a power represented in most cases by the political. We perceive the landscape as being the (re)presentation and the existence of the real in a multitude of relation systems rich in symbols. It is at the same time a frame of social life, of the individual's existence, of transformation and becoming. The cultural landscape is habituated as nature can be. It represents an ambiguity which inevitably leads to confusions or misunderstandings. This whole stage is monopolized by what many people call culture, which is, in a simple vision, nothing else but social life. A social life, which in the vision of Bourdieu is dominated by power, in whose

---

[171] Park 1926, pp. 1-14.
[172] After the book of the same author called *Landscapes of Power: From Detroit to Disney World,* published at University of California Press, Berkeley, 1991, in which she uses the concept of *creative destruction,* arguieing that the landscape is the most important cultural product of contemporary world.

practising all cultural symbols, from art, religion, behaviour, education, language, are components of some relations which lead to differentiation.[173]

The urban landscape has powerful social implications, being the stage of everyday life of millions of people. In such a context, power, one of the most important concept of social sciences, is the one that determines differentiation, relations and hierarchy. Without this way to manifest superiority one towards the other (either system or individual), the social discipline or subjection process cannot be produced. In the urban space this power can lead to classification of spaces, to social hierarchy and imposing economic mechanisms vital for the existence of a society. The making aware of the existence of a superior control mechanism over the individual means deciphering a symbols and relations capital, which define society and which are fundamental to politics and power.

The landscape is a symbol of power, a complex system in which spatial and social differences are mediated. Thus, the urban landscape reflects the way of thinking, the experience, the value system and culture of each group, individual or community, being a language which characterizes the modern society and emphasizes the defining characteristics of individual categories implied in modelling the urban space, such as architects, planners, investors, political decision factors and last but not least the citizen, the final user of this complex relation system. The cultural landscape can be considered a project of the political, in the context of the contemporary city, in which the understanding of this operational concept means knowing the economic, social and cultural processes, that define the urban space and its transformations in the last decades.

In a culturally rich environment, such as the urban space, the control over the cultural landscape is impossible. And this landscape of power is a political and unstable one, being under continuous change, dynamic as an existence form of culture. It is also a space which teaches us, a space of making aware of the individual's existence in the society, within a group or a community.[174] The human subject is integrated through relations and reports of power within the contemporary urban society, being a prisoner of the personal history

---

[173] Swartz 1997, p. 7. David Swartz wrote in *Culture and Power. The sociology of Pierre Bourdieu*: "the struggle for social distinction, whatever its simbolic form, is for Bourdieu a fundamental dimension of all social life.(...)Indeed, for Bourdieu, power is not a separate domain of study but stands at the heart of all social life".

[174] Tuan 2008, p. 102. Yi-Fu Tuan said in *Space and Place. The Perspective of Experience*: "the built environment clarifies social roles and relations. People know better who they are and how they ought to behave when the arena is humanly designed rather than nature's raw stage".

formed along decades of dual existence, from the wish of individuality to differentiating at the reality lead by isolation, fear, paranoia and rupture from community. The social consciousness of the individual existed under such an unexplainable paradox, like both approval and denial of the communist system existed. The communism was an ideology which was based on building an equal society, with no social classes, all goods belonging to the society as a whole, and individuals having the same social and economic statute. Socialism, as a concept, referred to a complex of ideologies and political movements which combated the individualism and defended equality and solidarity by implementing collective actions.

Therefore, modern urban life in post-socialist cities led to the apparition of two new experiences, the one of abandon and the one of loneliness, which led to serious identity problems of individuals. The post-modern world caused the early human fears, which in history led to the building of the fort as a defence system, to become urban fears. These are fears connected to a interior aggressor, due to the derangement of social order, of the relation between people and of the transformation of the urban landscape. At the same time, the century of speed and power of money, the globalization and the descendent trend of world economy determine us to start thinking about urban culture as not being totally dictated by money and power, but as a whole determined by the contradictions of the urban life. According to Sennett, the contemporary cities are cosmopolite, dense and somehow dangerous, being spaces of dislocation, deconstruction and disorientation. At the same time the contemporary city is a space of heterotopias, these very cultural differences being the ones that enstranges us from the other individuals or give us the feeling of fear and uncertainty in the urban spaces. Thus the mutual avoidance and the separation got to be survival strategies in the urban metropolis, which becomes a space of censorship and excessive control where panoptic strategies are possible. Therefore, in the 20th century the new way to observe and reflect about the city appeared as an exterior phenomenon to the individuals who live in it. The city is seen as a mirror of modernity, which determined us to reflect on the individual's condition as belonging to social groups bearing culture and generating identity. The term of mirror given to the city makes us think about Foucault and his heterotopias, where the mirror was a mixed space for it, being at the same time utopia and heterotopy, a "space without space" but which has a "retroactive effect"[175], as well

---

[175] Foucault 2001, pp. 250-260.

as about the ideal fort as imaginary city, which does not exist in sensitive space and time.

Illustration 10: The "Scanteii" House, built between 1952 and 1957 in Bucharest. It's destination was to accommodate the State's Publishing services. After 1989 it's name changed into "The House of the Free Press". It's architecture was inspired by Russian Leningrad Hotel and Lomonosov University buildings and is similar to the Palace of Culture in Warsaw, Poland. It was a symbol of power. The power of the written word in the Socialist regime. Image by the author.

Psychogeography and the cultural landscape

Along time and in different domains there are known intense preoccupations related to the study of the place and the experience of the individual in the urban space. In this context the cultural landscape is much more than just an image of a pace having a great influence on the individual's behaviour especially in the urban space. For a complete understanding of the concept several theorists appealed to, except the study of the urban image, the study of the senses and the way in which they influence the individual's existence in a city. Consequently in our process to present the main methods and concepts, which can lead to a complete understanding of the operative concept of the cultural landscape, we appeal to a relatively new and little known domain, the psychogeography, The father of this science is considered to be Guy Debord, and its birth took place at the beginning of the 50's in Paris under the influence of Lettrist Group, or also known as Letterist International. Thus, from the very beginning Debord defined psychogeography as being

> the study of the precise laws and specific effects of the geographical environment, consciously organized or not, on the emotions and behaviour of individuals.[176]

Merlin Coverley defined psychogeography as being

> a tool in an attempt to transform urban life[177],

a way to study the impact of the urban space upon the individual. Thus, an important characteristic of the psychogeographical analysis represents the act of walking[178] through the urban space. Thus the purpose is to overcome monotony and banality that the daily experience of the urban built space can bring. We are thus urged to look at the mysterious meaning of the city. Since the 19th century Thomas de Quencey has been practicing the observation methods of the city, which later were elaborated at another scale, in the 30's of the 20th century of the adepts of the surrealist current and in the 50's of the same century by the adepts of the above mentioned Lettris group. In the 60's situationalists called psychogeography a science of the derive, of the drift, of walking in the urban environment having a precise purpose, often motivated by a theoretical and scientific research or in other cases by a political motivation, not just a loafing driven by curiosity.

The same Merlin Coverley proposes us an exhaustive presentation of the way in which psychogeography came into being presenting many of the important actors of this process of coming into being of the above mentioned field. Among them we mention Iain Sinclair, or Thomas de Quencey, less known, or Michel de Certeau, Charles Baudelaire, Guy Debord, André Breton or Walter Benjamin[179]; we will refer to some of them later on.

---

[176] Guy Debord in *Introduction to a critique of urban geography*, online accessed on the site http://www.monoculartimes.co.uk/city-tours/psychogeography/urbangeography.shtml and appeared for th first time in 1955 in *Les Levres Nues No. 6*. This site was accessed on 18 August 2010, 18:59.

[177] Coverley 2010, p. 10. Quote "Under the stewardship of Guy Debord, psychogeography became a tool in an attempt to transform urban life, first for aesthetic purposes but later for increasingly political ends".

[178] Coverley 2010, p. 12. Quote "This act of walking is an urban affair and in cities that are increasingly hostile to the pedestrian, it inevitably becomes an act of subversion".

Another name which is worth mentioning is Will Self[180], an author whom Merlin Coverley gives as an example in his attempt to realize the evolution of the concept starting with Guy Debord up to the present; in fact he is considered the best example of the way in which psychogeography and the way to write and interpret the urban experiences have evolved. Many may look at the phenomenon Will Self as an anomaly of psychogeography by the way he writes and relates to everyday experiences. The diverse way of acceptance and understanding psychogeography is very evident in Will Self's writings and articles in *The Independent* newspaper. It is a natural thing that any evolution of a concept, such as psychogeography, which gets closer to the title of science, or cultural landscape, which is a developed operative concept together with cultural geography, should lead to new tackling and new methodologies once with passing of time.[181]

THE FLÂNEUR AND THE OBSERVED CITY

In 1863[182] the French poet Charles Baudelaire used the word "flâneur" in order to define the person who experiences the city, discovering it through walking, which became a new method of observing the urban space. Translated into Romanian the term means wanderer or tramp "the wanderer"[183],

---

[179] For a better understanding of Coverley's approaches, I reccomend visiting the following website, where Lee Rourke takes an interesting interview to mr. Coverley for the 3AM magazine in UK. The interview has been published in 3AM magazine on 10th of march 2007. link: http://www.3ammagazine.com/3am/psychogeography-merlin-coverley/ site accessed on:18th of august 2010, 13:54.

[180] His real name is William Woodward Self, born on the 26 September 1961 and he is a British journalist and writer.

[181] Self 2007, p. 11. Quote "Although we psychogeographers are all disciples of Guy Debord and those rollicking Situationists who tottered, soused, across the stage set of 1960s Paris, thereby hoping to tear down the scenery of the Society of the Spectacle with their devilish *dérive*, there are still profound differences between us. While we all want to unpick this conundrum, the manner in which the contemporary world warps the relationship between psyche and place, the ways in which we go about to task, are various".

[182] In the document *The Painter of Modern Life*, by Charles Baudelaire, online accessed on http://www.columbia.edu/itc/architecture/.../pdfs/.../Baudelaire.pdf in the translation of Johnathan Mayne appeared at Phaidon Press. p. 12. Quote "Be very sure that this man, such as I have depicted him – this solitary, gifted with an active imagination, ceaselessly journeying across the great human desert – has an aim loftier than that of a mere *flâneur*, an aim more general, something other than the fugitive pleasure of circumstance".

[183] According to the online English - Romanian dictionary http://www.dictionarenglezroman.ro wanderer means hoinar or pribeag.

"the stroller"[184] or "the stalker"[185]. The term is used strictly for the urban wanderer characterizing the critical attitude towards modern urban life, when the city (more correctly the metropolis) becomes suffocating and its knowing and even sensing its investigation in the meaning of flâneur is disturbed by the continuous and agitated activity. Thus the term flâneur is connected and associated with the term of mass. Before Baudelaire, Edgar Allan Poe wrote in 1840 about mass as being a symbol of the modern city. Both Baudelaire and Walter Benjamin would refer to E. A. Poe's writings in order to characterize flâneur. Baudelaire sustains that for flâneur

> the crowd is his element, as the air is that of birds and water of fishes. His passion and his profession are to become one flesh with the crowd.[186]

Even if he did not distinguished as a type of the American psychogeographer Edgar Allan Poe, the characters of his books characterize him as a forerunner of the European psychogeographers, managed to create a new type of the individual, the urban individual, who was at the same time part of a crowd, but he was also detached, a observer isolated from the crowd and the city, the forerunner of the inhabitant of the modern city[187]. In the works of the American writer the flâneur[188] type appears whom we later find at Baudelaire: a stroller who easily integrates in the mass and who is isolated by the very mass, a character who cannot be characterized and whose intensions are not clear, an individual who announces the apparition of a new city type, the modern city.James Werner[189] showed that the flâneur is a dull type difficult to be defined or analysed, but a versatile and flexible figure, who constantly ap-

---

[184] According to the online English - Romanian dictionary http://www.dictionarenglezroman.ro stroller means (1) persoana care se plimba sau (2) muzicant sau actor ambulant.

[185] According to the online English - Romanian dictionary http://dictionar-englez-roman.ro/ stalker menas vanator.

[186] In the document *The Painter of Modern Life*, by Charles Baudelaire, online accessed at http://www.columbia.edu/itc/architecture/.../pdfs/.../Baudelaire.pdf translated by Johnathan Mayne appeared in Phaidon Press. p. 9. Quote "The crowd is his element, as the air is that of birds and water of fishes. His passion and his profession are to become one flesh with the crowd". Accessed on 19 August 2010, 13.29 o'clock.

[187] In the document *Man of the Crowd* by Edgar Allan Poe, online accessed at http://etext.virginia.edu/etcbin/toccer-new2?id=PoeCrow.sgm&images=images/modeng&data=/texts/english/modeng/parsed&tag=public&part=all Quote "This old man, I said at length, is the type and the genius of deep crime. He refuses to be alone. He is the man of the crowd. It will be in vain to follow; for I shall learn no more of him, nor of his needs". Site accessed on 20 August 2010, 11.54 o'clock.

[188] Benjamin 1999, p. 420. Quote "dialectic of flanerie: on one side, the man who feels himself viewed by all and sundry as a true suspect and, on the other side, the man who is utterly undescoverable, the hidden man. Presumably, it is this dialectic that is developed in <<The Man of the Crowd>>".

peared in the theoretic works about modernity and postmodernity. Still defining flâneur is ambiguous, the individual with this characteristic swings from being a simple stroller on the cities' streets to being a detective, a real code breaker, whose role is to decipher the urban codes.

The activity any flâneur undertakes implies a complete understanding from the simple observation (apparently simple because all the other following activities impose observation to have been made correctly and not at all simplistic), which appeals next to the nobles sense, the sight, to all the other senses, such as smell or hearing. Another activity is reading, which is tightly connected to observation, it is in fact the device that offers the whole set of decoding rules. Reading is made both on space and the urban life, and on the texts, inscriptions, urban signs. Finally, another important part is the text production based on what has been observed, but not all are subjected to al these activities.

This type of individual has always been associated with the urban figure of the Parisian[190] of the end of the 19th century and the beginning of the 20th one. Thus, David Frisby[191] mentions Walter Benjamin, who refers to flâneur as being a social type characteristic of the Parisian after the revolution of 1830. For Baudelaire Paris becomes a book whose pages can be read only by covering all paragraphs, each of it representing a street. Thus the line resembles a labyrinth, each step of the stroller creates a special moment, and the streets attract him further. At the same time Benjamin considered that the city's streets lead the flâneur in a lost time, thus his present experience being correlated with childhood and the past experience. Streets open and offer the

---

[189] Werner 2004, p. 1. Cit. "One of the most fascinating figures to have appeared, disappeared and subsequently reappeared in the landscape of Western culture has been the flâneur, the strolling urban observer. (…) However, flanerie has by no means been relegated to intellectual or cultural obscurity, though it has languished there for extended periods in the nineteenth and twentieth centuries. With its emphasis on the discontinuities and dislocations of urban life, flanerie has made a significant impact on theories of modernity in general, and in some very specific ways".

[190] Benjamin 1999, p. 417 (M1,4). Quote "Paris created the type for the flâneur. What is remarkable is that it wasn't Rome. And the reason? Does not dreaming itself take the high road in Rome? And isn't that city too full of temples, enclosed squares, national shrines, to be able to enter *tout entiere* – with every cobblestone, every shop sign, every step, and every gateway – into the passerby's dream? The national character of the Italians may also have much to do with this. For it is not the foreigners but they themselves, the Parisians, who have made Paris the promised land of the flâneur – the <<landscape built of sheer life>> as Hofmannsthal once put it. Landscape – that, in fact, is what Paris becomes for the flâneur. Or, more precisely: the city splits for him into its dialectical poles. It opens up to him as a landscape, even as it closes around him as a room".

[191] Frisby 2007, p.31.

stroller a bit of the experience of each but through the filter of the personal experience the final point being his room. The city opens and closes at the same time around him like a room. Walter Benjamin goes even further saying that streets are dwelling spaces of the community, social groups and masses, being the space in which you learn and experiment. It thus passes from the flâneur type to the social group, the mass, which offers the individual the necessary air to unfold his activity [192], which, as Benjamin affirms, is planned.[193]

In his trial to analyse a series of motives from the works of Baudelaire Walter Benjamin inevitably comes to distinguish the concept of mass and affirm that mass is not characterized as being exterior to the poet in his works but that the author himself comes to identify with mass finding it hard to find clear references in his works and distinguish the frequent apparition of the motive of people mass[194].

flâneur being the type of the stroller at the end of the 19th century together with the industrial revolution and the changes brought to the urban and social life, he changes together with the environment he lives in. He has to accept and adapt to the city of the 20th century becoming a mental traveller, solitary and attached to the space of his room, which replaces the vital space of the city of the past in which he used to unfold his activity. A complete change of the individual's movement vector is being produced, which in the past happened in the order: room - urban street - city's exploration - again room and intimate space; now the rooms stays the total space in which flâneur makes his strolls, and the experiences become mental, the exploration of the city is being made only at a cognitive level. In the past the city used to close around flâneur as his room, becoming an intimate and protective space, which permitted him to explore the unknown, now the room opens, becomes a vast space of the city leaving place to happenings and mental experiences.

---

[192] Benjamin 1999, p. 423 (M3a,4). Quote "Streets are the dwelling place for the collective. The collective is an eternally unquiet, eternally agitated being that – in the space between the building fronts – experiences, learns, understands, and invents as much as individuals do within the privacy of their four walls".

[193] Benjamin 1999, p. 423 (M3a,2). Quote "The best way, while dreaming, to catch the afternoon in the net of evening is to make plans. The flâneur is planning".

[194] Benjamin 2007, p. 167. Quote "As regards Baudelaire, the masses were anything but external to him; indeed, it is easy to trace in his works his defensive reaction to their attraction and allure. The masses had become so much a part of Baudelaire that it is rare to find a description of them in his work. His most important subjects are hardly ever encountered in descriptive form".

It is what will be used by surrealists in their trial to discover the city by trips guided by the subconscious.

Surrealism and the experimental travel

We mentioned the term flâneur and made a short introduction in psychogeography enumerating several key characters who contributed to the development of this field. We will later on refer to the initiator of the surrealist current, André Breton, because though his theoretic works he helped defining the main concepts and directions, which led to framing and recognizing psychogeography as a subject and as a science. During the World War I André Breton was enrolled in the medical service of the army taking care of the wounded and helped to their recuperation. Psychologically this affected him so much, that after the war he was interested in psychology and the study of the subconscious, studying Sigmund Freud and the French psychiatrist Pierre Janet.

The social context after the World War I was of cultural pessimism, which led to a high interest in Freud's theories about human aggressiveness and fragility of human reason. Society was crumbled by a political and cultural crisis, which facilitated the interest towards the cultural movements before the war. Around the 1920's the anxiety and pessimism of the European societies led to the apparition of new radical artistic currents with major influences, which considered that the post-war reconstruction can be made only through a revolution[195].

André Breton has been considered the theoretician father of surrealism since 1924 when he published *Manifesto of Surrealism*. In this paper Breton gave a definition of the current saying that he was a supporter of a possible (de)composition of dreams and reality in a unique absolute reality, which he

---

[195] Löwy 2009, p. 22. Quote "In any case, this Marxism, (…) draws upon the subterranean current running through the twentieth century, beneath the immense blockades constructed by orthodoxy: Romantic Marxism. By this I mean a kind of thought which is fascinated by certain cultural forms of the precapitalist past and which rejects the cold, abstract rationality of modern industrial civilization – but which changes that nostalgia into a force in the battle for the revolutionary transformation of the present. All Romantic Marxists struggle against the capitalist disenchantment of the world (…), but in Andre Breton and the Surrealists the Romantic/revolutinary urge to reenchant the world through imagination finds its most striking expression".

called "surreality"[196]. This affirmation has been made together with a speech about dreams and referring to Sigmund Freud and the analysis of two worlds, the conscious one and an subconscious one, a rational one and a fantastic one. Breton presents a dual reality in which the state of waking up of the sleep and dream is an interference one. Through his writings Breton tried to present a series of realities of the subconscious, which he transposed in art through the study of dreams and the conviction that the domination of logic over the human mind has ended.

Surrealism was an artistic movement which acted between the two world wars and which shocked by the expression way of artists, either plastic artists, poets or fiction writers, having at the same time revolutionary aspirations. It came into being from Dadaism and was sustained by European artists, who tried to redefine the conventional notions of reality and subconscious by strange approaches of a dreamt, subconscious reality combined with presentations of animal instincts. Thus in the work of surrealist artists there are different themes in which sexuality is presented with the help of symbols placed in odd places even in the poems of Andre Breton, the activity of writing being compared to making love[197].

Besides the literature and artistic creation surrealists were guided by the wish to transform everyday life and replace the world existence with an extraordinary one based on a state of drift in which the perceptions of the individual over the surrounding world to be changed. Thus one of their practices was based on automatism which implied a certain action guided by the subconscious. This implied the writing and drawing or automatic painting as well as walking, strolling guided by the subconscious. Thus the individual journey on the city's streets was a dual activity both guided by the subconscious and transformed and modified by subconscious activities. This kind of walking, which in fact had no sense and no initial purpose but it was considered that it would lead to discovering some things and significations,

---

[196] In *Manifesto of Surrealism* online accessed under
http://www.tcf.ua.edu/Classes/Jbutler/T340/SurManifesto/ManifestoOfSurrealism.htm
Quote "I believe in the future resolution of these two states, dream and reality, which are seemingly so contradictory, into a kind of absolute reality, a *surreality,* if one may so speak. It is in quest of this surreality that I am going, certain not to find it but too unmindful of my death not to calculate to some slight degree the joys of its possession". accessed on 20 August 2010, 18.17 o'clock.

[197] In *On the road to San Romano* online accessed under http://www.surrealists.co.uk/bretongallery.php Quote "Poetry is made in a bed like love". Accessed 21 August 2010, 10.41 o'clock.

which otherwise hadn't been discovered by the process of guiding, led to the development of the term derivé, which was later used by situationalists.

For surrealists this act of drifting guided by the subconscious did not have results, which Breton refers to in his manifest. The automatism, which the supporters of surrealism based on, proved to be difficult and slow, and what was believed to be produced in the subconscious often came to be the product of a conscious thinking act. Thus, the politic and social context between the two world wars and the annexation of surrealists to the Communist doctrine led to losing some supporters of the movement and to the transformation of the prototype of the strolling individual, of the flâneur, which was to be defined by situationists in a character which declared the right to action in order to gain (again) the city, to whose destruction and transformation he was witness.

The model proposed by surrealists at the beginning of the 20th century take a new shape in the 21st century in what we call today the experimental tourism. The term was used by Joel Henry, a French journalist, in order to define a new type of tourism, which he promoted by the very grounding of an organisation called Latourex, described by the founders as "a laboratory of experimental tourism"[198]. The same Joel Henry is the author of the book enmtitled *Lonely Planet guide to experimental travel*, which appeared in 2007, in which he describes over 400 ways to travel, which are different or maybe strange, but some of them known as practices of investigating the space and the city by professionals. There are approach ways of some urban trips, no matter if you are a visitor of a city or if you are passing by.

Even if some consider this description of some unconventional visiting methods as beign strange or even pathetic and with no success, the author states that the elaboration of these methods are based on concepts and methods used by surrealists at the beginning of the 20's of the 20th century[199]. This way to discover a city, visit it and investigate it is directly connected to the way in which surrealists considered automatism as a basic principle in exploring the city through the individual's subconscious. He becomes an explorer, a detective a mental traveller trough a new or already known city, ap-

---

[198] In the interview of Frank Bures taken to Joel Henry, the founder of Latourex, online accessed under http://www.worldhum.com/features/travel-interviews/jol_henry_the_dean_of_experimental_travel/ on 21 August 2010, 14.33 o'clock.
[199] In the online interview under http://www.worldhum.com/features/travel-interviews/jol_henry_the_dean_of_experimental_travel/ Quote "It's a new way to travel based on scientific or pseudo scientific rules. Traveling under such constraints turns travel into a kind of game. So experimental travel is something between a game and travel".

pealing to all his senses and his entire knowledge gained so far in order to be able to create the mental image of the visited city. Mentioning the knowledge and training level and the culture of the individual implicated in this process we have to mention that there are unconsciously approached, the individual not being able to describe or express what he saw only using a certain set of tools, which we can call languages or rules, with the help of which he deciphers what he observed, and which he acquired due to his professional training, of the personal experience, of the past and present experiences and states.

Out of the over 40 experiments we mention some, which have influences based on concepts and theories of the supporters of surrealism. Thus one of the ways to discover the city with the eyes closed and guided by another person, called by Joel Henry "cecitourism" or on the website *Lonely Planet*[200] appeared under the name of "blind man's buff travel". In this way you are obliged to discover the city with the help of the other senses except the sight, but which through the own filter of thinking and the past experiences can form a mental image of the visited spots based on sounds, smells or the texture of the touched surfaces. This way of experiencing the urban space leads us to David Serlin's work, *Disabling the flâneur*[201]. In this work Serlin tries to redefine the limits connected to the way in which the term flâneur is understood through the analysis of the way in which blind people perceived space using a photography from 1937 with Helen Keller[202] at Paris. The description of the photo in which Keller and Polly Thomson, her company, were looking in the shop windows on Champs-Elysees, presents the way in which Keller were presented the shown cloths, thus being able to virtually experiment[203] (imaginary) the charm of the shop windows on the boulevard of the French capital.

---

[200] This information and these details about each trip way described by the author of th book is foud online under http://www.lonelyplanet.com/experimentaltravel/contents.cfm. Accessed on de 21 August 2010 17.18 o'clock.
[201] Serlin 2006, pp. 193-208.
[202] Helen Keller was born in 1880 in the United States being a politic activist and writer. When she was 19 months old she got sick and since then she hasn't been able to hear or see, being the first blind-deaf person who gained an academic diploma at Perkins School of the Blind.
[203] Serlin 2006, pp. 194-195. Quote "Their apparent delight in and longing for the consumer goods that have captured their attention is marked not only by the message that Keller comunicates directly into Thomson's hand, (…) but also by the reflexion of both women mirrored in the window's glass that seem to haunt the shop's interior and our perception of the event. Indeed, the sumptuous display behind glass serves as a kind of visual analogue for Keller herself, who experiences the clothing in the shop window not through tactile means but though virtual projection as mediated through Thomson's gaze and subsequent description".

At the same time in sustaining the argumentation of this way to discover the city we mention the notes of Walter Benjamin in *The Arcades Project*, in which he presents a quotation of Georg Simmel referring to the weight of the situations in which sight is more often used than hearing in the urban daily life. Thus he states that the one that sees but does not hear is under a greater stress than the one that hears and cannot see[204]. Thus the bustle of the modern city, the whole urban life, which unfolds in front of the observer's eyes, can be tormenting if he can not hear at the same time, while according to Simmel, the blind person who relies only on hearing is considered less worried about what happens around him. "Aesthetic travel" is called the journey type in which the individual, armed with different devices such as camera, paper and pencil or any other registration device, can discover a city taking pictures of the urban furniture or of certain details of the buildings without taking pictures of the street perspectives, or writing a poem or some rows in every square he visits, in order to finally create a new album of his journey. There is described also the travelling way based on the automatism which the surrealists have promoted, called "automatic travel", in which the traveller is urged to get free of all the prejudices and the thoughts and let himself led by the subconscious and the moment impulses and the immediate experiences based on the experimented sensations offered by new discovered spaces. Under the name of "contretourism" it is described the way in which the individual, being next to a landmark or a location of a certain interest, will be very attentive to the adjacent spaces of that location, taking pictures or making notes about the close buildings, while the opposed perspectives of that objective does not pay any attention to the objective itself.

The flâneur of the end of the 19th century and the tourist of the 20th century seem to have common roots. Completing the above mentioned the flâneur can be considered the ancestor of today's tourist judging after the way in which every one escapes out of the everyday life and transcends into a ephemeral world through a trip of a past dream, wish or even a moment's impulse for discovering something new. Wearing, Stevenson and Young referred to the flâneur type of the modern city as a man typology, who not only observes urban life but as a real archaeologist is involved in digging out collective myths and dreams of modernity[205]. But we are not directly interested

---

[204] Benjamin 1999, p. 433 (M8a,1). Quote "Therefore the one who sees, without hearing, is much more ... worried than the one who hears without seeing. This principle is of great importance in understanding the sociology of modern city. Social life in the large city ... shows a great preponderance of occasions to *see* rather than to hear people".

[205] Wearing 2010, p. 7.

in the tourist while trying to settle an investigation way of the cultural landscape, but we consider that the incursion in what experimental tourism means and the knowledge of its putting intro practice are at the base of any type of landscape investigation, which directly involves the senses and appeals to the experience of every person and to his knowledge gained over time.

The one who investigates the cultural landscape is a descendent of what the theorists of modernity called flâneur; he is an urban detective, a tourist of the concrete world, a mental traveller in a space, which is a mental construction: the city. It is a character who investigates staying detached from the investigated object[206], who appeals to his own set of rules and who uses his own decoding language of the urban symbols and the landscape. The senses and thoughts based on assimilated knowledge and the experience are the tools[207] he uses in his trial to break the codes and bring some more knowledge. Each individual having or not the necessary training and knowledge necessary for this kind of investigation is a flâneur, a researcher of the urban space.

THE NEW URBANISM AND THE SITUATIONISTS

Remaining in the area of psychogeography we will appeal to theories which tried to redefine urban life and urbanism. Between the wars, through the Carta from Athena from 1933 the group CIAM defined within the 4th congress the main directions, which the modern urbanism was based on. At the same time the bases of the fictional city were laid. This new kind of approach in urban planning and projection led to a series of critics, and in 1953 Ivan Chtcheglov presented in his *Formulary for a New Urbanism* the principles for redefining urbanism, which criticized the banalization, which appeared in the urban life. The rigorously conceived, monotonous, ridiculous and too

---

[206] Wearing 2010, p. 8. Quote "But while the signs and symbols he searched for through his use and observations of space may have been those of the collective, the flâneur remained detached from what he observed. He chose not to engage with either the people or the places he visited, thus his way of seeing and being in space was highly idiosyncratic and individualistic – it was not interactive".

[207] Heidegger 2006, p. 270. Quote "Noi spunem ca un context ustensilic ne înconjoara. Fiecare ustensil individual este, potrivit esenței lui, un ustensil *ce serveste la ceva*, la calatorie, la scris, la zbor. Fiecare ustensil are o legatura imanenta cu acel ceva *pentru care* este ceea ce este".

academic spaces (we have to mention here John Brinckerhoff Jackson's attitude towards modern architecture) led to critics from the supporters Lettrist Group, such as Chtcheglov. Even if in his work we can observe that fact that he was delirious, the argumentation of the 19-year-old youngster for reinventing urbanism and the appeal to action towards modern architecture are bitterly affirmed.[208]

Chtcheglov becomes a critic of the modern technology and of the changes it brought in the experience and urban life saying that "we don't intend to prolong the mechanistic civilizations and frigid architecture that ultimately lead to boring leisure"[209], being a supporter of the sublime and the picturesque experiences in contrast with the rational and the mathematic spaces of the urbanism and modern architecture[210]. At the same time he considered that new architecture is at the base of new civilization, outlining three key points as being fundamental in defining a new civilization, such as a new concept of space and time and human behaviour[211], proving that the notion of relativity, which is so often in modern language leads to the hypothesis that a certain experimental aspect of the new civilization can be adopted. This experimentation is the answer to a mental disease, which Chtcheglov considered as being responsible by the triviality, which conquered the life of the individuals[212]. Observing Chtcheglov's arguments we can easily deduce the situation-

---

[208] In *Formulary for a New Urbanism* by Ivan Chtcheglov accessed online under http://www.bopsecrets.org/SI/Chtcheglov.htm. Site accesat în data de 24 august 2010, ora 13.10. Quote "All cities are geological. (...) We move within a closed landscape whose landmarks constantly draw us toward the past. Certain shifting angles, certain receding perspectives, allow us to glimpse original conceptions of space, but this vision remains fragmentary".

[209] Chtcheglov Quote "we don't intend to prolong the mechanistic civilizations and frigid architecture that ultimately lead to boring leisure".

[210] Chtcheglov Quot "architecture is the simplest means of articulating time and space, of modulating reality and engendering dreams. It is a matter not only of plastic articulation and modulation expressing an ephemeral beauty, but of a modulation producing influences in accordance with the eternal spectrum of human desires and the progress in fulfilling them. The architecture of tomorrow will be a means of modifying present conceptions of time and space. It will be both a means of knowledge and a means of action".

[211] Chtcheglov Quote "A new architecture can express nothing less than a new civilization (...). Anyone thus has the right to ask us on what vision of civilization we are going to found an architecture. I briefly sketch the points of departure for a civilization: a new conception of space (a religious or nonreligious cosmogony); a new conception of time (counting from zero, various modes of temporal development); a new conception of behaviours (moral, sociological, political, legal; economy is only a part of the laws of behaviour accepted by a civilization)".

[212] Chtcheglov Quote "A mental disease has swept the planet: banalization. Everyone is hypnotized by production and conveniences – sewage systems, elevators, bathrooms, washing maschines".

ist theories. The way in which the city was transformed by architects tributary to the modernist movement was criticized, feeling the need of an urban revolution. Le Corbusier is criticized in the document which militates in favour of a new urbanism of Chtcheglov's, who considered that the model of Corbusine architecture lead him to suicide destroying any rest of joy[213]. At the same time, such as situationists, surrealists were criticized for the modern architecture, Andre Breton referring to his architecture Le Corbusier as being the most brutal creation of an automatism.

We discussed about situationist theories because many of the concepts launched by them are mentioned and discussed. We do not mention here only the intellectual elite and the theorists of the city, but we refer to concepts such as spectacle or defalcation or drift. These, especially show, are operative concepts which continue to appear in the contemporary urban theory.

Guy Debord is the father of psychogeography, who continued what presituationists started, defining psychogeography and stressing out the way in which urban space influences the individual's behaviour. He was a supporter of a delimitation of different areas of the city based on the derive technique, not taking into account the urban morphology or the architecture of the place and he believed in a future in which architecture and urbanism will be at anybody's hand as tools in creating space and the new cartograms of the city[214]. In 1957 the Situationist International was grounded to which supporters of presituationist groups such as Lettrist International and International Movement for an Imaginist Bauhaus or CoBrA adhered. Thus, the new created group detached from the artistic preoccupations and adopted a political legend, which had a strong Marxian influence. The main activity, the creation of situations with practical and theoretical purpose, was the most radical aspect of the whole activity of the organization, which has its roots in the ac-

---

[213] Chtcheglov Quote "Some sort of psychological repression dominates this individual (…) such that he wants to squash people under ignoble masses of reinforced concrete (…). His cretinizing influence is immense. A Le Corbusier model is the only image that arouses in me the idea of immediate suicide. He is distroying the last remnants of joy. And of love, passion, freedom".

[214] Guy Debord in *Introduction to a critique of urban geography*, online accessed under http://www.monoculartimes.co.uk/city-tours/psychogeography/urbangeography.shtml and appeared for the first time in 1955 in *Les Levres Nues No. 6*. Accessed on 24 August 2010, 17:53 o'clock. Quote "the production of psychogeographic maps, or even the introduction of alterations such as more or less arbitrarily transposing maps of two different regions, can contribute to clarifying certain wanderings that express not subordination to randomness but complete insubordination to habitual influences (…). This sort of game is obviously only a mediocre beginning in comparison to the complete construction of architecture and urbanism that will someday be within the power of everyone".

tions of surrealist groups, which were dissolved by the end of the World War II.

Guy Debord became almost a dictator of an organization, which is a radical one and whose purpose was to transform urban experience. This is how psychogeography and practices adopted by the situationalists were defined such as derive and détournement or the unitary urbanism, which were to be defined by Debord. Consequently the term détournement was a shortcut of the syntagma "détournement of pre-existing aesthetic elements"[215] and represented an integration of artistic productions in a social environment and a superior structure. The term derive meant an experimental way of behaviour[216] by the individual's passing through different states during the urban journey coming to live different states.

We have to mention an interview from 1983[217], in which Henri Lefebvre admired situationists and the way in which their relations evolve, saying that he knew Guy Debrod well and respected the supporters and the founder of the group. He mentioned also the group CoBrA, which was mainly formed of architects and which he considered as being between surrealists and situationists, from which the revolution wanted by the situationists started and which was inspired by one if his books. Thus Lefebvre mentions how architects of the CoBrA group believed in a change of everyday reality with the help of architecture. Lefebvre affirms that the use of situationists to create situations was connected to his theory referring to moments, but they considered that they take everything to another level. What Lefebvre called moments, situationists called situations. This denomination of new situations has always remained ambiguous and unclear, but a series of experiments have been made by the forerunners of the Situationist International and the members of CoBrA in cities like Amsterdam and Strasbourg. Their purpose was to create bounds between different parts of cities, which were spatially separated, which gave birth to the derive technique.

---

[215] Coverley 2010, p. 94. Quote "short for: détournement of pre-existing aesthetic elements. The integration of present or past artistic production into a superior construction of milieu. In this sense there can be no situationist painting or music, bur only a situationist use of these means. In a more primitive sense, détournement within the old cultural spheres is a method of propaganda, a method which testifies to the wearing out and loss of importance of those spheres".

[216] Coverley 2010, p. 93. Quote "a mode of experimental behaviour linked to the conditions of urban society: a technique of transient passage through varied ambiances. Also used to designate a specific period of continuous deriving".

[217] Ross 2002, pp. 267-285.

The derive technique was prefigured by the surrealists through their wanderings guided by the subconscious. Debord wanted to differentiate the derive technique from Breton's automatism as he did not agree with Freud's theories, which represented the base of surrealist techniques. Thus derive became a technique in order to explore the existence forms of every day and which tried to annul the principles and techniques of the after war Capitalism's techniques. Their revolutionary spirit was shaped clearer and clearer and Debord's motto was "ne travaillez jamais" (we never work). This comes up from Lefebvre's interview, who affirmed that Debord had no wealth, he led a miserable life but having a special intellectual air[218].

Nieuwenhuys, ex-member of CoBrA and then member of Situationist International was the one who initiated the first ideas and worked at the theoretic concretization of a new city, a utopia which would frame the principles of a situationist architecture and of a situationalist city. Thus the utopia called *New Babylon* was created. Its main principle was disorientation[219], which implied the creation of a confusion in the spatial hierarchy, which proposed obstacles and the creation of spaces with incomplete geometries as well as elements with different textures, materials and different colours, even transparent. Thus the wish was that the created space should not be concretely differentiated or subjected to o fictional division into zones, the space being free, usable in the manner of any individual, not making the strict difference between public and private. Everything was a kind of continuation of the ideas presented by Chtcheglov in his *Formulary for a New Urbanism*.

Nieuwenhuys militated for the creation of another city type for another life way. He criticized the way in which the contemporary city of the situationists had transformed. He considered that the city no longer offered the adventure spirit which the inhabitants needed[220]. Nieuwenhuys' argumentation we observe a disapproval of what modern architects created considering that the

---

[218] Ross 2002, p. 268. Quote "I remember a hole night spent talking at Guy Debord's place, where he was living with Michele Bernstein in a kind of studio near the place I was living on the rue Saint Martin, in a dark room, no lights at all, a veritable ... a miserable place, but, at the same time, a place where there was a great deal of strength and radiance in the thinking and the research".

[219] Sadler 1999, p. 143. Quote "To enter into the New Babylon labyrinth was to submit to what Constant called its <<principle of disorientation>>".

[220] Nieuwenhuys 2002, pp. 95-96. Quote "We require adventure. Not finding it any longer on earth, there are those who want to look for it on the moon. We opt first to create situations here, new situations. We intend to break the laws that prevent the development of meaningful activities in life and culture. We find ourselves at the dawn of a new era, and we are already trying to outline the image of a happier life and a unitary urbanism – urbanism made to please".

way, in which cities have been conceived needs to be changed by bringing the social part in front. We can observe the wish to create a utopian, visionary city, which prefigured the evolution of metropolises and megalopolises of nowadays.

All these happened in a key moment in the history of humanity. His work was written in 1959, a period in which the spatial course[221] between the United States and Russia started. In 1957 the satellite Sputnik was launched and in 1959 the capsule Lunik by Russia, and in the same year Americans launched the capsule Pioneer IV two months after Lunik. The race for conquering space began, and the moment in which the first man reached the moon happened only a decade later. In the same year in the United States the first microchip was launched by Texas Instruments[222]. Thus what so far had been a fantasy came to be reality. What later represented the base of modern life and technological and communicational evolution was realized based on microchips. In the same year, after a few months from the appearance of the microchip, IBM presented the first computer of small sizes (comparing to what they had at that time) and at a lower price, the forerunner of personal computers. It was the time of revolutions and changes. It was the time in which situationalists were talking about collective creativity, about the creative forces a city has. Among these culture was considered the main one. They militated for a cultural revolution and they criticized the way in which culture had to suffer because of individualism[223]. It was the moment in which community was brought to the main rank by the promoter of urban evolution, of the change of the way of urban life. There were created what we call today creative cities; the need to change to create cities, which continuously adapt and reinvent themselves.

The unitary urbanism of situationists presents new doctrines in the same way in which it criticizes the functionalist urbanism. Another character, of the same importance as Debord, is Raoul Vaneigem, whose theses on urban everyday life brought a series of drastic commentaries towards urbanism. He compared it with a nightmare. For Vaneigem the loss of identity in contem-

---

[221] Kaplan 2009, pp. 72-76.
[222] Kaplan 2009, pp. 76-84.
[223] Nieuwenhuys 2002, p. 96. Quote "Our domain is thus the urban network, the natural expression of a collective creativity, capable of understanding the creative forces being released with the decline of a culture based on individualism. To our way of thinking, the traditional arts will no longer be able to play a role in the creation of the new environment in which we want to live".

porary cities was considered a disease, which threatened the capitalist world [224]. This identity crisis made the derive technique differentiate from the flâneur one. It was not a simple stroll through the vast and meaningful spaces of the city. Tom McDonough[225] said that the difference between flâneur and derive was the very tactic situationists brought as an answer to the technique of automatism surrealists were using. Thus a new way of living in the city was needed.

Even if part of their concepts and techniques used in order to redefine urban experience disappeared as a practice and are only studied in works of urban theory, the situationist concept of spectacle frequently reappears in contemporary architecture and urbanism. According to situationalists cultural and social theories are bases of communication, and communication is the key element in social life. But the capital society reduced everything to a one-direction communication, in which everything around becomes turns into a spectacle, and the individual is a spectator. Guy Debord starts his work of 1967 *The Society of the Spectacle* affirms that life in a modern society is an accumulation of spectacles[226] which are nothing else than results of the interhuman social relations[227]. At the same time Debord considered that the weakest part of the concept of spectacle associated to modern life represents the inheritance brought by the continental philosophy, which was based on the concept of vision, sight as the most important and used sense[228]. In Debord's theory on this is based the whole evolution of contemporary society. The decrease of distances, the increase of the speed, with which cultural changes are produced as well as the way the values of a society dominated by

---

[224] Vaneigem 2002, p. 121. Quote "the capitalist training of space is nothing but training in a space where you lose your shadow, and end up losing yourself by dint of seeking yourself in what you are not. An excellent example of tenacity for all professors and other licensed organizers of ignorance".

[225] McDonough 2002, p. 257. Quote "For the situationists, however, the derive was distinguished from flanerie primarily by its critical attitude toward the hegemonic scopic regime of modernity".

[226] Debord 2002, par. 1. Quote "in societies where modern conditions of production prevail, life is presented as an immense accumulation of spectacles. Everything that was directly lived is now merely represented in distance".

[227] Debord 2002, par. 5. Quote "the spectacle is not a collection of images; it is a social relation between people that is mediated by images".

[228] Debord 2002, par. 19. Quote "the spectacle inherits the weakness of the Western philosophical project, which attempted to understand activity by means of the categories of vision, and it is based on the relentless development of the particular technical rationality that grew out of that form of thought. The spectacle does not realize philosophy, it philosophizes reality, reducing everyone's concrete life to a universe of speculation".

consumption was contested led to the creation of a scene in which the spectacle of everyday life became the preferred piece of a consumerist public[229].

Consequently a series of contemporary critics, such as Jonathan Crary, discussed upon the fact that Debord did not make a historic analysis of the term spectacle but simply places the moment of the birth of spectacle's society in a precise time, without explaining the choice of a certain year. Thus Crary proposes a series of explanations of the way in which Debord refers to modernity of the 20's as being the moment of the birth of spectacle's society. Besides the mentioned facts, among which the way in which several discoveries in physics in 1927 influenced the evolution of television[230], the prize award of the film *The Jazz Singer* in the same year 1927 which was the first film with synchronized sound[231], and politically and ideologically during this period fascisms and Stalinism were born, we have to mention the influence which the first manifest of surrealism had in 1924 (and that Crary mentions in the end of his essay), and which changed the way in which art was seen in the public space and the way in which urban experience was to be enriched by the new described techniques[232].

Situationists were some marginalists not being accepted or well-seen, revolutionaries[233] who drew only critics and their methods were based on what many would have called a simple play. Consequently how else can we end this chapter than with what stefan Guga affirned on the blog of de urbana:

> today nobody can be situationalist any more.[234]

But we consider their methods and contributions to the way of perceiving the city important for the study of the contemporary cultural landscape, in which affectivity, the mental side and memory are important components, which led

---

[229] Debord 2002, par. 165. Quote "capitalist production has unified space, breaking down the boundaries between one society and the next. This unification is at the same time an extensive and intensive process of banalization".

[230] Crary 2002, pp. 457-458.

[231] Crary 2002, pp. 458-460.

[232] Crary 2002, p. 464. Quote "but the same year, 1924, the first surrealist manifesto suggests a very different aesthetic strategy for confronting the spectacular organization of the modern city".

[233] Nieuwenhuys 2002, p. 114. Quote "The <<foundations>> in preparation for an experimental life, of which the SI program of unitary urbanism speaks, are at the same time the places, the permanent elements of a new kind of revolutionary organization that we believe to be inscribed in the order of the day for the historical period we are entering. These foundations, when they come to exist, cannot be anything but subversive. And the future revolutionary organization will not be able to rely on instruments less complete".

[234] Stefan Guga on the site blog urbana http://socasis.ubbcluj.ro/urbanblog/?author=8 . Accessed on 2 September 2010, 12.00 o'clock.

to a complex and fundamental concept, which was taken out of the rurality with which it was defined in the works of the American geographer Carl Sauer.

Taking into account what we have presented so far and sustaining what stefan Guga affirmed we need to mention the way in which the discussion about situationists reappeared at the academic level in the last years. Thus Erik Swyngedouw considered this phenomenon as being ironical, which reappears at a turning point in the evolution of urban society when terms such as creative cities and innovation systems are more and more present in intellectual speeches, and virtual space, the cyberspace redefines human experience. What was once considered revolutionary and radical got to gain the respect at the intellectual level after almost forty years[235].

---

[235] Erik Swyngedouw, in *The strange respectability of the Situationist City in the Society of the Spectacle.* Accessed under http://eprints.ouls.ox.ac.uk/archive/00000904/ and initially published in *International Journal of Urban and Regional Research* 26(1):pp. 153-165, 2002. Quote "It is ironic that Archigram, Utopie and most notably, the S.I., have found academic and cultural respectability at the beginning of the 21th century, a respectability and acclaim that is pinned upon the spectacular representation of its creative moments, thus confining it to the spectacular commodified representation of these projects also silences, ignores, and forgets (in a short of pre-meditated amnesia) the profound theoretical and political insights that underpinned these excursions into new forms of urban practice and living". Accessed on 14 September 2010, 10.40 o'clock.

From daily life to virtual community

The evolution of everyday life of the way in which the individual perceives the urban space changed a lot together with the technological evolution and the increasing use of computers and the Internet.

The urban experience received thus a new dimension, and the next step in its evolution was the creation of a second life[236], which thus produces a double environment, in which every individual can live and explore the virtual space as in the real one. Everything becomes a virtual spectacle. It is a way to nourish a schizophrenic mind of a person for whom the need for spectacle and change of the active role he has in the real life leads to behaviour changes and adaptation to new techniques to experiment the urban environment, to socialize and integrate in the virtual community. Thus, the 21st century represents the moment of (re)birth of the society of spectacle, which virtually took place, the spectacle being in a built world, a world of information and technology, a world in which creativity and innovation are key terms, and the cultural globalization is the one which settles the scenery of the urban spectacle, being at the same time the exclusive producer.

Virtual space: Heterotopy and tool in the creation and investigation of the cultural landscape

We will continue the above mentioned mentioning the heterotopy of Foucault or those other spaces which Lefebve mentioned. In order to understand Foucault's term heterotopy, as we will see further one, on much help will be Peter Johnson's vision upon the other spaces. Knowing Foucault's original

---

[236] Second Life is a virtual world which was created in 2003 by Linden Lab. The phenomenon second life has developed enormously, and its evolution from a simple online game to a real social phenomenon expecially in advanced societies led to the creation of an advanced environment in which many companies moved their businesses online, where they can gain a lot of money, or schools use it as a learning systemand development of social relations. For a better understanding we propose studying the document *Second Life: An Interactive Qualitative Analysis* uder http://research.educatorscoop.org/SL.IQA.site.final.pdf . Accessed on 14 September 2010 13.12o'clock.

text Johnson's contribution is important in understanding the term heterotopy as spaces opposing the usual. At the same time he presents the way in which Foucault avoids giving examples for the term heterotopy the very notions, which sustained the term of utopia in order to underline the distinctive character of the concept[237].

At the same time the sociologist Teresa Davis, from the University of Sydney, Australia, mentioned Lefebvre's wish to include space (as a philosophical concept) in the cultural dimension[238] of production. In his article he relates to the terms "third space" and "heterotopia". In analogy with the heterotopical space of the child, which is both real and imaginary, Teresa Davis leads a study on a virtual group of ex-university colleagues, who meet again after twenty years. These members are from different places, living on different continents and although they have the same cultural background adopted different cultures in the places in which they chose to live, which made their group be a multicultural one. Thus, the virtual space becomes a heterotopy, being that space which exists (for each individual of the group space exists through the order terminal of his computer), but also they are in an imaginary space, outside the real space (it is meant the user's interface in which conversations are led, files are being transmitted and photos are being exchanged)[239].

Taking Teresa Davis's experiment as the first example in our discussion referring to virtual spaces a new existence way of social space, we will continue our argumentation through the analysis of the way in which urban social experience moves to a virtual level. We cannot forget about how almost every day the computer and the virtual world are never-missing, without them the activity in contemporary life being unimaginable. Thus, local communities move to the virtual world. And talking about community we have to accept its role in defining the cultural landscape. This is how through the study of cultural landscape we came to its aspect of heterotopy, through which we are transferred into a virtual world. Eric Gordon and Gene Koo elaborated a study referring to a pilot program, which was being unfold in Boston, United States in which urban communities are implied in the process

---

[237] Johnson 2006, p. 81. Quote "Foucault's account of heterotopia, however playfully presented, remains briefly sketched, prosivional and at times confusing. (…) It is also significant that although he does refer back to it briefly on two occasions, Foucault never returned to this spatial framework in any explicit or sustained manner. This open-ended and ambiguous analysis has in turn provoked many conflicting interpretations and applications across a range of disciplines, particularly sociology, human geography and architecture".

[238] Davis 2010, p. 662.

[239] Davis 2010, p. 666.

of urban planning through the virtual world of technology[240]. The pilot program entitled Hub2 was initiated in order to permit members of different communities to actively imply in the process of urban planning through a virtual environment of the MUVE (Multi User Virtual Environment) type and having as a main platform Second Life. Thus the voice of community is heard and directly implied in the process. With other words community is directly implicated in the development of the cultural landscape by accessing the virtual world Second Life and using 3D advanced technologies[241]. There are other proofs of using the virtual environment in the study of the urban. Thus Justin Hollander and David Thomas talk about a virtual planning[242]. In a case study it is shown how Second Life was used as a virtual environment for the students who used design courses[243]. The advantage that the virtual environment offered compared to the usual way to study the urban environment was the easiness with which students could visualize the proposed sites for the project. The negative reactions towards this study were mostly, as the authors describe[244], about the way in which the environment Second Life uses 3D creation techniques, which as students affirmed were different from the programs with which they were used[245].

Taking into account what Yi-Fu Tuan affirmed that place is a lived space and can be affectively and mentally expressed due to past experiences and experienced by the individual[246], at the level of community and the social

---

[240] Gordon 2008, pp. 204-221.
[241] Gordon 2008, p. 205. Quote "Thus, Hub2 primarily aims to nurture local communities that can (a) understand and analyze what makes public places precious to them; (b) rationally deliberate over the design of public spaces; and (c) powerfully assert their communal vision within the larger democratic dialogue".
[242] Hollander 2009, pp. 108-113.
[243] Hollander 2009, p. 109. Quote "While the classes used Second Life in different ways, each required students to utilize the program as a virtual design studio. (…) Students attended face to face classes and used the Second Life environment as a virtual urban laboratory".
[244] Hollander 2009, p. 110. Quote "The biggest challenge we faced in teaching with Second Life was confronting the fact that this <<virtual>> world was real in many ways. On a few occasions, students and staff involved in both classes were harassed by other avatars, for which we responded by excluding those outsiders from the virtual classrom space".
[245] Hollander 2009, p. 110. Quote "Students in Physical Planning and Design had little prior experience in 3D modeling and were largely intimidated by the difficulty of creating objects in Second Life. Students in Planning in the Gaming World had, on avarage, considerable experience in 3D, but they too were quite frustrated with Second Life because of its unique proprietary modeling system, which they found limited and awkward compared to more familiar tools".
[246] Gordon 2008, p. 206. Quote "Place is experienced space. It is what happens when geographic space takes on meaning of any sort – as an object of memory, desire, or fear. Place can be produced through happenstance (the space of a kiss), through narrative (the space of childhood that is persistently articulated with story), through familiarity (the space one lives

groups space has another signification. This is a system, a sum of all the individuals' spaces experienced and expressed in a personal and unique way, which at the social level were expressed by Eric Gordon as being place-worlds[247]. They are those spaces which regardless of their signification for the individual at the level of community they have another cumulative signification, which defines a common language of decoding the meaning of that space, which should make it accessible to the whole social group. The purpose is to create a common vision upon the spaces in which they live, and in order to obtain this result the virtual environment was of great importance.

Consequently the virtual space of Second Life offered the subjects a place in which the ideas about the change and adaptation of the urban space could be put into practice[248].

A NEW TYPE OF FLÂNEUR. THE ONE OF VIRTUAL SPACE

We all know what a computer game is, moreover many of us, especially young people, got to play such games. Studying the virtual space we will analyze the modern cosmopolitan flâneur, the one that once with the evolution of technology changed its tactics and the action place: the virtual space. This is where the proof of evolution of the modern flâneur competes from; the virtual space is no longer a transposing into the cyberspace of the urban space. The virtual explorer has the chance to discover a series of different spaces which the one at the beginning of the 20th century did not have the chance. Thus through the computer game, either online (on the net or multi-user) or single user the contemporary flâneur discovers new places, new virtual cities, interesting locations or even the cosmic space (through games such as Star Wars Galaxies). At the same time they have the chance to play games in which the main purpose is to administrate and lead a town (like Sim City) or to handle a whole family such as in the game Sims.

---

each day), or through representation (the space of art or advertising). This identification with place is an important method of organizing personal experience and social actions".

[247] Gordon 2008, p. 206. Quote "Places become placeworlds when their inhabitants imbue them with meaning through communicative action – the reasoned deliberation, with the goal of mutual understanding, that animates all lifeworlds. Whether a street corner, a favourite hangout, a neighborhood, or a playground, places are particularly well-suited for establishing common purpose among groups of people".

[248] Gordon 2008, p. 212.

We reached the moment in which we have to accept the fact that nowadays gaming, the technique of the computer games became an important activity in the life of many young people (even elderly people). Thus the anguish produced by the urban space, which is in continuous change, the dangers we are exposed to in a contemporary city as well as the wish of many people to escape from everyday life leads to a virtual urban flanerie[249]. The old wanderer wanders on the streets of a city created of 0 and 1, his senses being almost completely annulled. All the individual's experiences take place at a cognitive level, in the imaginary, while leading his avatar (created by him according to his own wish, who many times embodies an almost perfect character, who has no weakness of a real individual) on the streets of an unknown city or a city created by himself.

Bart Simon characterized this virtual flâneur as resembling to the one described by Baudelaire transposed in the informational area. Some kind of a swat, as it is described, a workaholic wishing to escape from his routine and explore new locations in a virtual digital environment[250]. From the practice of everyday life it is thus observed how the evolution of contemporary society determines a distancing of the individual towards the urban space and their implication is less and less. The capitalist city comes to resemble to an urban jungle out of which the individual can escape only in the virtual world. On the other hand this very urban space becomes the place of experimenting the feelings of the cyberspace, when some people forget to make the difference between real and virtual and consider the real urban space as being their action place similar to the virtual one.

Thus the way to understand and perceive the exterior space, either urban or not, is influenced by the way in which the individual lives the actions from cyberspace. James Carrier clearly transposes the main problems that come up in understanding the space by the individuals[251], considering that the main

---

[249] Simon 2006, p. 64. Quote "My approach, which is both conceptual and methodological, is to understand digital gaming in terms of an intersection of four kinds of broader problematics that inflect our sociotechnical lives in the early 21st century, that is, to view games and gaming simultaneously as central nodes in the organization of contemporary leisure culture, computer-mediated interaction, visual culture, and information societies".

[250] Simon 2006, pp. 62-63. Quote "This 21st century flâneurie is no less gendered, raced, and classed than the urban Victorian precedent mythologized by Baudelaire. Hard core cyber-flâneurs tend to be geeks, technological elite with the knowledge, skills, and resources to uproot themselves from their workaday lives to travel the Infobahn in search of vicarious pleasures in foreign lands".

[251] Carrier 2003, pp. 5-23.

contribution in this field was brought by Tim Ingold[252]. Referring to his contribution Carrier clearly presents the way in which people are in relation in the outer space. Some of them consider themselves as being the centre of what is going on and see the world as a sphere, and those which are distant and uninvolved are those who see the world as a globe[253]. This is how the ones of the second category are the prefigured type of the flâneur by Baudelaire and Poe in their works. The type of man who is both part of the crowd and also distant towards it is the one who looks upon and studies the crowd distantly from outside. Furthermore, once the individual enters the virtual space, he takes part to a different existence that is a plural one[254]. In this way, the virtual space becomes the ground where the individual has multiple identities and even bodies. This opportunity gives the virtual flâneur the chance the experiment the space through different virtual identities, thus being differently perceived by the virtual neighbours.

The contemporary flâneur is active in a world in which the real combines with the imaginary in the virtual world. Its everyday experience doubles with a virtual experience, which opens the access to locations, which otherwise would have been impossible to visit[255], being thus a tool in the investigation process and space research.

---

[252] Tim Ingold was born in 1948 and he is a techer of anthropology at Aberdeen University of Scotland.

[253] Carrier 2003, p. 6. Quote "At one extreme are people who are, and who see themselves as being, enmeshed in those surroundings; people who, Ingold says, see the world as a sphere in which they and their practical activities are at the centre. Such people do not distinguish the cultural and the natural realms in any very clear way. At the other extreme are people who see themselves as being distinct from those surroundings; people who see the world as a globe, outside of which they stand and which they observe at a distance. Such people draw a distinction between the natural on the one hand, and the social and cultural on the other".

[254] Taylor 1999, p. 439. Quote: "Online virtual spaces open up the construction of self and body in dramatic ways. Users do not simply have one body and one identity while online, but at times inhabit a space in which they perform several, and often in complicated configurations. In fact, the moment you enter a virtual environment you immediately have at least two bodies: a corporeal one and a digital one".

[255] Harrison 2009, p. 80. Quote "Individual virtual settlements like SL provide a crucible within which one can witness the origins and development of settlements which mirror those from the actual world, to which we would otherwise not have access".

THE EVOLUTION OF THE STUDIED CONCEPT. CONCLUSIONS

After 1990 we can observe a growing interest among researches towards the urban, and the theoretic models were influenced by Marxist doctrines, so that the concepts of cultural landscape launched by Sauer and Jackson were considered „ altogether too evasive about systematic forces of political economy in mainstream capitalist America and in answering the question of who and what, in fact, create urban and rural environments".[256]

Phil Hubbard affirmed regarding Trevor Barnes's vision upon the evolution of the theory in geography and the way in which it has influenced the understanding and interpretation of the cultural landscape since Sauer's first theories, thus:

> Trevor Barnes offers a similar definition, suggesting that geographic theory need not provide logical relations, rules of causation or empirically verifiable statements. For him, what is crucial is that a theory expresses a phenomenon through a new vocabulary and syntax which changes the way people interact with it (in terms of how they view it, or study it, or practise it).[257]

Consequently, while the concept was evolving and was subjected to the changes brought by the structuralist, post-structuralist, deconstructivist or post-modernist doctrines, the authors tries to move off the "rurality" with which the operative concept of cultural landscape was associated at the beginning, and they used new terms, proper to the contemporary philosophical discourse such as *space, spatiality* or *social space*. The dialectic of the social space of the social space was on the first place in the works of theorists like Henri Lefebvre, Roland Barthes or Michel Foucault, some of them being influenced by Marxist doctrines. Evolution was inevitable and definitely justified, and the first concepts became the victims of the critics of the generations of culture theorists that followed. The term culture has always been ambiguous, the same as the one launched by Sauer for the first time, that of *cultural landscape*. Thus the theorists before the war among which we name Sauer and Jackson, to a certain extent, saw culture as an independent but responsible complex of human behaviour, and starting with the first part of the

---

[256] Wilson 2003, p.16. Quote „altogether too evasive about systematic forces of political economy in mainstream capitalist America and in answering the question of who and what, in fact, create urban and rural environments ".

[257] Hubbard 2006, p.10.

20th century there were adopted new theories and ideologies which changed the course of the study of landscape and multiply the meaning given to culture.

For geographers the interest towards the study of landscape and culture was shown especially at the level of theories and studies regarding the definition of the terms space and place, terms which have an ambiguity as great as the cultural landscape. The theorists of social sciences and philosophers were those for whom defining space and place were on the first place in their researches, but geographers had also a special interest. They introduced the emotional side of the study of space with interest in the relation types in which the built environment imposed upon everyday life.

Thus, knowing the evolution of the concept in cultural geography as well as the application of certain investigation methods of the urban environment such as psychogeography are essential to the study of cultural landscape. At the same time the virtual environment and the development of global information networks and the Internet led to the apparition of some virtual worlds, which are important in sociologic and urban studies, although as psychogeographic techniques they started from a game. What we experiment today as Second Life was first a simple computer game, but either if we accept this or not, the apparition of the virtual world negatively or positively influences our way to experiment the urban space.

Thus the operative concept of *cultural landscape* represents a relation system, one of power together with economic, social and political forces. Thus *culture* and *the landscape* are sources of power and sometimes of domination, and combined the two form relations which gave birth to some processes which (re)produce spaces and meanings.

Every city, like every individual, has a personal identity, which is historically determined, as well as in time and space. In this context it can only be about a value system, which constantly interacts with the urban system and which determines the cultural landscape, identity representing a way of relationating between the different evolutional stages in the development of the urban system. Thus, taking into consideration the above mentioned, the contemporary city represents in a symbolist interpretation a spatial and social cohesion. It is an environment which cannot offer protection, being extremely vulnerable and amplifying panic. The social cohesion is thus compromised due to its cultural dimension. According to what was mentioned above, the urban cultural landscape can be understood as a sum of *relations* and *tensions*, a process in essence, which determines the contemporary public space as a space of reflection in which the individual can exist without feeling the manipulation caused by the communicational flows, which standardize the contemporary urban experience.

The post-socialist city is in essence a symbolic space, our mental construct in which the culture is the most complex system of relations and power, in conjunction with economic, social and political forces. It indicates a unique way of seeing the real and living it in a space that is not only an instrument of the politics and power, but is also a scene for life, experience and representation. Thus culture and landscape are sources of power and sometimes domination, and combined, the two form relations which give birth to processes which (re)produce spaces and meanings. We can argue that the landscape is an imagined product of the society that still has a connection with the reality but plays the role of a desired product.

Illustration 11: View over downtown Bucharest by night. Image by the author.

In conclusion, we can argue that the contemporary city is dealing with a series of challenges that need to solve a very important issue that is in essence the pursuit of happiness, and the urban planning and cultural planning are the instruments to be used in order to achieve this goal. By understanding and getting involved in the process, the individual needs to learn how to deal with the urban cultural landscape.

The visions of the real we were trying to shape in this paper by passing through different concepts from different disciplines are in a certain matter ways of pursuing happiness, of imagining the city and creating the sense of a place in the city. The study of the cultural landscape we believe to be of critical importance for a city, in order to understand the messages and symbols within it, to impose our thoughts and ways of imagining it, to achieve happiness and self realization.

We really hope this to be a very promising start in the study of the aspects of modernity in the urban cultural landscape of Romanian medium and small towns, in order to understand the transformations of the post-socialist urban areas and to bring new methods and ways of studying and understanding the operative concept of cultural landscape. Therefore, as Bridge and Watson stated,

> different theoretical approaches tell different stories which purport to some kind of truth about cities but which are themselves only one way of understanding the complexities that constitute a city. There is no one narrative of a city, but many narratives construct cities in different ways highlighting some aspects and not others[258].

---

[258] Bridge, Watson 2000, p. 14.

FROM THEORY TO PRACTICE. A COMPREHENSIVE VIEW

CASE STUDY: CULTURAL PLANNING AT A REGIONAL LEVEL

GENERAL PRESENTATION OF THE REGION[259]

Illustration 12: View over the Tarnava Mare river valley from the high hills of Medias, in central Romania. In the background are the Fagaras Mountains. Image by the author.

Illustration 13: View over the small town of Medias and the Tarnava Mare river valley. Image by the author.

---

[259] The present study was conducted in 2007 for the master's degree. By that time, the lack of information on a regional development level determined us to create the study based on the information found on the websites of the local authorities. It was created as a model in the study of cultural planning process. The SWOT diagram was realised after a series of interviews and personal observations in that region, as for more then 25 years I had the opportunity to live there (in the small town of Medias).

Tarnava Mare Valley is located in the middle of Romania, in Development Region no.7 – Center. The surveyed zone includes five urban settlements situated along the river, beginning with Sighisoara as eastern point to Blaj as western point and the neighbouring rural settlements in between. Initially being part of the Tarnava Mare County (in the inter-war period)[260] and Tarnava Mica county, the territory now includes the administrative parts of three counties: Alba, Sibiu and Mures. By analyzing the attached maps on the websites, one can distinguish Tarnava area as an ethnographical region in Transylvania. Also, comparing the maps of the abolished counties of Tarnava Mare and Tarnava Mica one can notice that the two of them, existing in the inter-war period, were very accurate delimiting the represented area, which determines us to consider that the administrative demarcation, at least in the regard of those two counties, was very near of the ethnological and cultural one. This takes us very close to the domain of expertise of this study. We have here a very proximate example of cultural region which, in the past, encompassed two administrative regions or counties.

The three middle towns (Medias, Sighisoara and Blaj) and two small

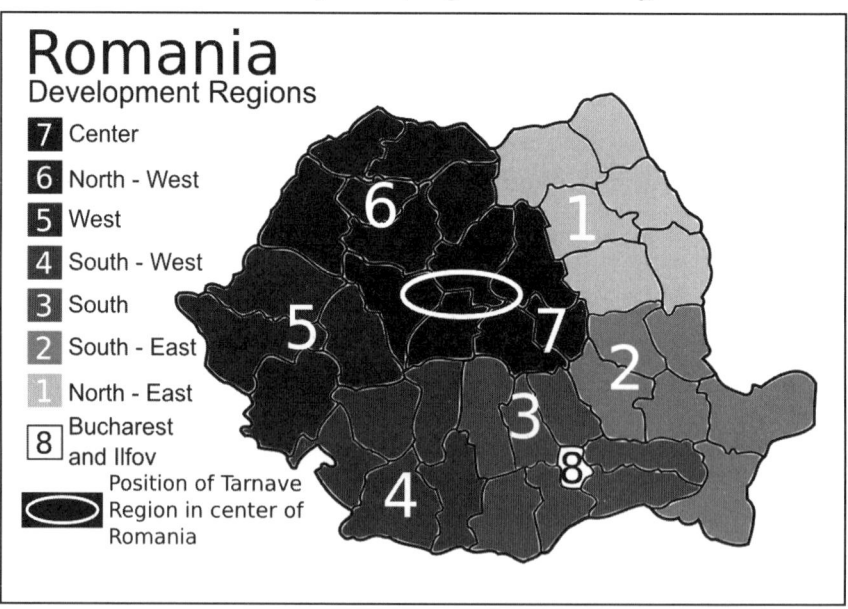

Illustration 14: The eight Development Regions of Romania. Map designed by the author.

---

[260] The data used for this description is found on http://romaniainterbelica.memoria.ro/ .

Diagnosis

Tarnava Mare Valley represents a compact area regarding the landscape, historic past and demographic profile and is, in the same time, rich and diversified in potential tourist and ethnographic patrimony.

The urban network neighbouring the river is characterized by different towns uniformly distributed along the river, with populations varying between 55.153 inhabitants[261] (Medias) and 5.142[262] (Copsa Mica). Those towns are situated at the crossroad of two important urban areas: Targu Mures and Sibiu.

From a geographical point of view, the urban population had a fast growth during the communist period (especially in the 60s and 70s) as a result of the appearance of some big industrial sites. But after the revolution, urban settlements were characterized by negative values of the natural and migrational growth as a result of the economical restructuring and the new laws regarding properties.

The area is crossed by the national roads DN 14B that links Blaj and Copsa Mica and DN 14 that links Copsa Mica and Sighisoara. At Sighisoara is the point where European road E60 crosses the region, road which links the capital to the northwestern part of the country. Along Tarnava Mare Vally between Sighisoara and Blaj the main railroad 300 from Bucuresti to Oradea also crosses the area.

Regarding the natural resources, the area abounds in natural gas deposits. Specific to the highlands relief are the crops of grapevine and fruit-trees. Tarnava Mare river has a low flow and, being high polluted, the usage of it's waters is limited. The tourism potential of the area is given by the existence of the numerous fortified saxon churches and by the fortresses in Sighisoara and Medias. Another high tourism potential is on one hand, in the wine-growing area, as the vineyards of Jidvei and Tarnave are included in the tourist route *Wine Road of Transylvania* and on the other hand, the thermal resort of Bazna.

---

[261] According to Wikipedia, in 2002 the number of inhabitants in Medias was of 55.153. website http://ro.wikipedia.org/wiki/Media%C8%99 accessed on 17th october 2007, 10.00 am.

[262] Data collected from the local authorities website www.copsa-mica.ro . Website accessed on 17th october 2007, 10.05 am.

Tourist routes from the area of the fortified saxen churches are poorly signalized along the access roads, and tourist information points are missing from most of the places from the studied area.

The accommodation capacity is also limited, fact that denotes the poor development of tourist activities compared to the development potential of the area.

From an economical point of view, the urban population was and still is preponderantly involved in the primary and secondary sector, the tertiary sector which consists mostly of tourist and proximity services, is still developing. The processing industry, which is the primary economical activity of the urban establishments, had recorded a decrease in the last 18 years, as a result of the foreclosure of some industrial giants, being affected especially the towns of Copsa Mica and Medias. This fact caused many social problems and the leaving of some important industrial sites, which contributed to the demographical decline of the area. Copsa Mica had been declared under-privileged area and by the facilities given to the employers it was tried to be given a support for the economical conversion and revival of the town.

DISTINCTIVE COMPETENCES

Tarnava Mare river is the pivot of a relatively unitary zone in regards of the landscape, and of economical, demographical and cultural potential. The urban settlements are uniformly situated along the valley, and the small between them practically generates a linear and sedate urban development, fact that makes so that no one of them to become an attraction pole for the other ones. There are many exchanges between the communities along the river, that were generated by the transportation axes development (especially railroad axes) and, for a period of time, there were two distinctive territorial administrative units – Tarnava Mare and Tarnava Mica counties – which gathered the urban and rural settlements from each side of the river.

The studied area is situated in the same time at the crossroad and at the margins of some important growth town poles from the region: Cluj Napoca, Targu Mures, Sibiu and Brasov, but without having a very pregnant influence from any of those. This very fact can be seen as an advantage, taking in consideration the possibility of benefiting from the development of all these four growth poles and also facilitating the area population's access to more complex services that are available in bigger towns (for example, specialized medical services, studies and university education). In the same time, this context stimulates and facilitates the urban settlements along the valley to become a kind of growth engine for the neighbouring rural settlements.

Tarnava Mare Valley consists of a great etno-cultural, patrimonial and natural diversity that means an important tourist potential insufficiently turned into an advantage. The value of the tourist sites that are in the area is also validated by the fact that some of them were included in the UNESCO world heritage. The intangible cultural patrimony can be identified all around the area, with some concentration differences as some categories are mostly identified in the urban area. Cultural events regard many domains, especially in the urban area, from exhibits of art and crafts to communications, symposiums and forums. The existence of ethnic minorities leads to a strong cultural diversity in many fields, fact that makes local communities to be more aware of the specific cultural and linguistic identities. In urban areas, a high interest for cultural activities can be observed along with an increase in the importance of cultural industries. In rural areas, traditional means of expressing were better preserved, and in the same time were stimulating contemporary creativity and intercultural dialogue.

Another important characteristic of the studied area is it's centrality in relation to the national territory. Doubled by an appropriate transport infrastructure, it's positioning in the middle of the county can become an extremely important advantage in the effort of attracting potential tourists, investors and even inhabitants. This strategic settlement can be an important advantage as a European railroad corridor had already been schemed along Tarnava Mare Valley. This area's positioning along the electrified main railroad is an advantage for the towns it passes through over the other settlements in the area, fact that confers them greater importance as local economical nods (for example, the main railroad passes through Sighisoara but not through Targu-Mures, a county capital, and also the link between Sibiu and Medias is made through an un-electrified railroad).

It also should not be neglected the industrial's activities degree of development or, rather the tradition of the industrial function in the area, fact that implies a specific training of the labour force and a sum of edilitary equipments suited for large dimension industrial sites. For example, the town of Copsa Mica is tooled up with freight train terminals and power supply equipment that can handle Mw's.

Main disfunctionalities and their effects

The studied area is served by a low quality road infrastructure with a defective connectivity to the main transport routes that links the neighbouring urban poles. In the same time, as railroad transportation is regarded, also Copsa Mica is considered to be a railroad node, the connections with the main urban settlements under which's area of influence the studied area is, are indirect, also existing unmodernized railroads. Thereby, excepting the railroad that goes along Tarnava Mare Valley, the studied settlements are poorly connected to the neighboring urban poles, which lead to tourist and commercial traffic deviation to other routes. This turns in a real disadvantage for potentials investors in the area. For example, the options of transport from Sibiu to Sighisoara by train (that should probably be the main tourist axe of Transilvania) takes between 2h30min and 5h, changing route at Copsa Mica, for a distance of around 95km.

The bankruptcy of some big economical agents brought unemployment to alarming rates, to the abandonment and degradation of some important industrial sites and contributed to to the decline of the urban population. This economical and demographical decline had also been aggravated by the lack of a branch of small and medium enterprises that would have undertaken a part of the dismissed agents. Nowadays, urban settlements rely on several large enterprises (for instance, Medias rely on enterprises as Romgaz and Transgaz, the national gas companies), fact could aggravate the social problems if this enterprises would enter in bankruptcy and if there would not be a constant involvement of the authorities in sustaining economical activity's diversification and the growth of small and medium enterprises sector. The quality of the environment was and still is seriously affected by the industrial activities in the area, especially in the case of the towns of Medias and Copsa Mica, with direct influences on public health and the attractiveness of the area. Water and air pollution and the quality of the landscape are affected by abandoned industrial giants and could be an impediment in the exploitation of area's agro-tourist potential.

Tourism, as potential economical activity that could contribute to the revitalization of the area, is poorly developed, once because of the above mention causes (mainly transportation infrastructure's dysfunctions and pollution problems) and also because of authority's deficiency in making a common effort for stimulating local initiatives, for endowing the sights with the needed infrastructure and unitary promotion throughout the area. Moreover, as a mirror for the lack of or for the low development of tourist traffic in this area, stands the defective communications infrastructure, as the network of mobile telephony does not cover a great part of rural settlements. Without the necessary interventions, the natural and cultural patrimony is continuously degrading and the potential interested tourists in these attractions go to other touristic areas.

Possible development strategy

Taking into consideration on one hand the above identified problems and on the other hand the significant potential of the area, we believe that a development strategy that would emphasise the advantages and minimize the identified fears, bazed on the partnership and efforts of implied local authorities, could lead to significant positive results in a medium time horizon.

Tarnava Mare Valley should become a preferred transit area for Transylvania, an attractive, creative region, easy accessible for tourists and investors, hospitable and comfortable for its inhabitants.

The actions of the public authorities should be oriented towards improving and modernizing transportation infrastructure, facilitating the access in the area along the river and to rural settlements adjacent to it. In that direction, PATN, Transport Section, already forecasts area's connection to the future highways that will pass alongside Sighisoara, through Sibiu (TEN-R) and alongside Alba-Iulia (TEN-R). These connections will be made by express roads and four-lane roads. Also in Medias the modernization of a combined transport terminal is proposed (for intermodal transport facilities). Also, the current main railroad no.300 will be transformed in a double-lane railroad with a traveling speed of over 250km/h, that will be a part of 4 Pan-European Corridor. An important accent will be attributed to the modernization of the national and regional roads that link the rural settlements with the towns, as their labor force is mostly directed through urban settlements along the river and to the modernization of the roads that have tourist attractions along them.

The diversity of economical activities will be supported along with attracting investors for the revival of industrial activities in area's urban poles. This will increase the number of jobs available and will eliminate the risk of dependency on a single industrial branch or company. At the same time, the authorities will encourage the development of small and medium industry sector and will sustain retraining programs for the adults that were affected by the foreclosures.

Tourism development will be another important point advanced for public authorities' agenda. Will be taken into account tourist enhancement in the areas that had already been exploited: Sighisoara, fortified saxen churches, tourist space exploitation in the areas that are poorly exploited in this respect as Blaj and Medias, and also the development of alternative form of tourism (such as the spa resort in Bazna, wine-growing tourism, agro-tourism). A first step in this respect would be to take up a partnership between rural and urban settlements as a tourism potential for developing strategies and projects of common interest in promoting the area, building facilities and tourist information points for tourist attraction zones, sustaining entrepreneurial initiatives in this field.

Also, investments will be made in raising life quality and area attractiveness as means of combating the demographical decline of the area. In this respect, initiatives will be sustained for modernizing public spaces and facilities, housing improvement, modernizing health and education infrastructure, stimulating cultural activities, sustaining care services development and amelioration the quality of the environment.

Implementation

Of course, a strategic development plan of Tarnava Mare area can not be accomplished without the involvement of local public authorities from the area, without their cooperation and without consulting all the factors involved: economical agents, non-governmental organizations, academic environment, political parties and citizens.

The development strategy must be assumed by decision makers and reflected in the urban plans and in the multi-annual budget predictions. Furthermore, as it implies long time projects, political will and thus including strategic objectives on the political agenda of the decisional factors, requires continuity between elective terms.

The initiatives proposed by this strategy can be directly assumed by local public authorities from the studied area and can be materialized in the activity plan for the possible associative structures "intercommunity development association" type that local towns could form or can be transformed in founding lines through which local public authorities could sustain other types of institutions such as non-governmental organizations, educational institutions or medical units.

As financing is involved, as a result of the observed disfunctions, local authorities budgets are far exceeded over the need of investment in the area. A favourable context is given by many financing opportunities available for the next years through structural funds. Operational programs by which local public authorities might request funding for the proposed projects could be:

Regional Operational Program, through:

Priority Axe no 1: *Local and regional infrastructure improvement,* for initiatives regarding modernizing the infrastructure in fields as education or health

Priority Axe no 2: *Local and regional tourist development*, for initiatives regarding local tourism potential

Priority Axe no 3: *Sustainable urban development*, for initiatives regarding urban spaces and facilities revival and also reducing social problems

Human Resources Development Operational Program, especially through:

Priority Axe no 2: *Connecting lifelong learning with labor market*, for retraining and rehabilitation programs of labor force.

Operational Program for Increasing Economic Competitiveness, especially through:

Priority Axe no 1: *An innovative production system*, for initiatives meant to sustain small and medium industry sector and entrepreneurship.

Priority Axe no 2: *Research, technological development and innovation to enhance competitiveness*, for the modernizing initiatives, upgrading and diversification of economic activities in general and industrial activities in particular, from the studied area.

Priority Axe no 2: *Information and Communication Technology (ICT) for private and public sectors*, for the initiatives related to modernizing and improving management systems, communication and promotion, involving both public and private sectors.

Transport Operational Program, especially through:

Priority Axe no 2: *Modernization and development of land transport infrastructure to ensure access to TEN-T,* for studied area connection to transport networks of European interest.

Priority Axe no 3: *Modernization and development of national interest transport infrastructure,* for modernizing roads linking between localities from the studied area and nearby main urban poles.

Transport Operational Program, especially through:

Priority Axe no 1: *Expanding and upgrading water and wastewater systems,* for water quality improvement projects for Tarnava Mare River.

Priority Axe no 2: *Development of integrated waste management and rehabilitation of contaminated historical sites,* for initiatives of rehabilitation of abandoned industrial sites.

A MODEL FOR THE REGION

Here we are arriving at the last part of this study, where we elaborate on a cultural planning model for our proposed objective: Tarnava Mare Valley creative region. The whole approach at the beginning of this paper finds his finality in this last chapter, where we try to sketch a model and a methodology for implementing the principles of cultural planning in the chosen region. By this, we answer the main research question raised in the outset. With the risk of exceeding the estimated allocated space for this paper, we will give a brief presentation of a cultural planning model, of the guiding principles and priority axes of the proposed strategy. We consider that a more elaborated model could once again exceed the number of pages already achieved.

VISION, MISSION AND GUIDING PRINCIPLES

Vision:
The region of Tarnava Mare Valley bears a lot of history, having its own cultural identity. It would be the engine of economic development and welfare and shall be a creativity and inovation support through knowledge.

Mission:

The goal is to preserve, protect and suport cultural identity in the region, for present and future generations.

GUIDING PRINCIPLES	VALUES
ESSENTIAL VALUE OF CULTURE	A strong cultural identity represents a base for society's prosperity, development and adaptability at global changes. Culture is what defines our identity, enriches our way of living and it's a support for economic prosperity.
CULTURE AND QUALITY OF LIFE	Culture is a measurement tool for our way to exist as a society. Participation in cultural activities enriches our life as individuals or community, leads to social inclusion, to self-esteem enrichment and broadening each one's horizons.
SOCIO-ECONOMIC DEVELOPMENT	Culture investments lead to economical and authorized capital growth. Cultural industries contribute to economic regeneration in urban and rural areas alike. It must be recognized that cultural integrity, artistic quality and professionalism are essential to economical stability.
CULTURAL DIVERSTITY	The existent multiculturalism in the area, indicated by various ethnic groups that had populated the region over time, leads to a strong cultural diversity. The identities of every single ethnic group should be recognized and protected.
THE RECOGNISED VALUE OF THE PROFESSIONALS OF CULTURE	Proper development of cultural resources and using them effectively can only be done by the involvement of domain –skilled, recognized individuals
CULTURE, EDUCATION AND CONTINUING EDUCATION	It is important for the community to know the natural and cultural heritage and to develop its own talents artistic skills. Educational institutions of all types and libraries assume an important role in preparing future individuals involved in creative and cultural process, and investments in this field should be sustained at a central level.
ACCESS TO CULTURE	Every inhabitant and visitor of the region has the right to free access to cultural activities and resources. Culture professionals, residents of the region, are entitled to have their access to cultural markets ensured locally, regionally, nationally and internationally.
CULTURAL PARTNERSHIPS	Individual, community, regional, national and also international partnerships are encouraged between agents, institutions, freelancer artists that are involved in cultural process.

Strategic directions:

NO.	NAME
STRATEGIC DIRECTION 1	recognition and support for professional artists
STRATEGIC DIRECTION 2	creative communities and regions
STRATEGIC DIRECTION 3	creative education
STRATEGIC DIRECTION 4	creative labor force and developing jobs in cultural sector
STRATEGIC DIRECTION 5	preserving the tangible cultural heritage

STRATEGIC DIRECTION 6	intangible cultural heritage preservation and care
STRATEGIC DIRECTION 7	cultural and creative industries
STRATEGIC DIRECTION 8	cultural tourism
STRATEGIC DIRECTION 9	creative cultural research and new ways of information

These strategic directions, as we have named them, are priority axes of the elaborated strategy and they focus only on the cultural sector. They represent a frame of cultural planning, following that for each particular case several documentation steps to be made in order to achieve the proposed goal. The guiding principles are the ones that determine the frame in which the study will be done. In this case, 8 guiding principles have been chosen on which to elaborate a cultural planning. To achieve the proposed objectives, data referring to cultural sector should form a solid database as a base of SWOT analyses, identifying the mission and vision for each direction and putting a diagnosis. Taking into account that the main goal of the paper is to establish if cultural planning can be an indispensable process in developing a strategy for development, we referred to the strategic that we consider the most important for the development strategy of a cultural, ethnographic and historical region such as of Tarnava Mare. Among those listed above, we consider the most important to be: SD5 – preserving the tangible cultural heritage, SD6 – intangible cultural heritage preservation and care, SD7 – cultural and creative industries and SD8 – cultural tourism. Of these, SD7 has a high degree of novelty, being able in the same time to contribute to economic growth in region and at cultural tourism development and even at cultural heritage conservation. However, we could admit that SD2 – creative communities and regions can be of equal interest with SD7.

Conclusions of the case study

Along history the idea according to which culture is a form of adaptation to natural environment was stated. In the same context of determinism, culture was understood as a form of social life. Thus we have underlined the *obtained* character of culture. Culture is a process of learning and (re)production as factor answer factor. Culture represents the distinctive attribute of human condition, of not being a closed or perfectly stable entity. In the study of cultures it must be taken into consideration that they are in the same time different and alike and identifying differences and similarities is the result of studies and tests and differ according to the chosen scale for every mode of approach and research.

Our study brought to the conclusion that cultural planning, as a process of development strategies, is indispensable in the idea that keeping local cultural identities is needed. In the same time an important accent is put on cultural diversity and on encouraging multiculturalism in a Europe that risks loosing its identity.

The discourse on regions and cultural regions is essential in substantiate a framework of study, understanding the types of regions and of cultural regions in particular. Even if a clear delimitation of cultural regions hasn't been accomplished in this paper, it must be into consideration that essentially any region is a cultural region, a region bearing culture that can evolve through culture. Culture is certainly an element that explains many things but in the same time offers just a partial explanation of the way that people think or act. This also implies other explanatory elements as political, economic, social, mental or biological ones that can not be ignored but which can be interpreted in cultural terms.

But nowadays we are in a particular context, a „cultural moment" as we have named it in the book. In the context of globalization, culture and its derivates gain more weight. Social theories are more and more based on cultural terms in order to overcome the visions that suppress cultural and identity differences. Thus, European Union cultural politics are starting to make their presence more and more felt and the necessity of introducing them in the development processes appeared around early 90's.

A rethinking and renewal of these policies is needed in order to establish a favourable legal frame for their implementation. Problems as preserving cultural landscape, keeping and preserving cultural patrimony started to appear on the tables of decision-making bodies all over the world.

We are on the verge of a new beginning in spatial planning in which cultural dimension will be the most important and notions as creativity and innovation acquires new dimensions. The role of culture in economic development of regions and towns and also in regeneration processes is essential and leading. Cultural planning slowly makes its way through other planning types and culture becomes, in a broad sense, a notion that refers to collective identity. In this way, we have a picture in which world cultures stand side by side and culture becomes synonymous with society. Not least, the process of

cultural planning, the strategies of cultural policies and regeneration might become:
- Interdisciplinary and inter-cultural through good cooperation of those involved in their development.
- Much more critical and competitive by recognizing the dynamic character of culture that characterize a given space.
- Much more sensible from a cultural and historical point of view, through a better understanding of history, economical realities and cultural representations of a space.

Workshop essay. A good practice example

Remixing Architecture

In June 2008 I got by chance an e-mail from a colleague architect form Slovakia, Katarina Bohacova, who participated last year in the workshop from Mechelen, Belgium. Thus I found out about Re:mix, a company from Bratislava, which intended to organize an international architecture workshop. The problem was that at the same time I was about to go, at least this is what I thought then, to ISSP 2008, International Summer School of Photography, which was held in Ludza, Lituania and to which I had already been accepted. Thus I had to choose between the two passions of mine, photography and architecture. This essay is a clear proof that I chose the second one.

Presenting the theme

Those from Re:mix, Katarina Bohacova and Martin Berezny, two young and talented architects, proposed in this workshop an urban study of the district Petrzalka, situated in the South-West of Bratislava. From the beginning I had found the idea interesting as they described the area in the e-mail as being famous for its concrete apartment blocks.[263] They described it as being one of the most densely populated districts in Central Europe.[264] I suddenly thought about cities like Cluj-Napoca or Bucharest. Indeed there live here over 117,000 inhabitants, a pretty large number related to the entire population of Bratislava, of about 430,000 inhabitants.[265] Because of the high criminality rate the district is also called the Bronx of Bratislava, as here are most of the

---

[263] Quote from the short description of the project we had to do: "Petržalka is famous for its concrete apartment blocks built hastily in the socialist era to deal with the housing shortage".
[264] Bratislava Projects at MIPIM 2007 – Petržalka City (PDF) p. 8. City of Bratislava (3 January 2007). Retrieved on January 23, 2008. "Petržalka City will definitely change the face of the largest and most densely populated housing estate in Central Europe: the network of grey prefabricated buildings will be transformed into a fully-fledged town".
[265] The district's surface is of 28.7 km².

drugged people and drug dealers according to the authorities (78% of the inhabitants having middle and superior studies, a high percentage compared to other districts in Bratislava)[266].

Petrzalka was grounded, at least on paper, in the year 1969 as a result of an international contest organized by the authorities; the construction was started in 1977. The work for the contest project has started for the Slovaks since 1956, being the first great project after war. The big problem in the area was the marshy ground, which put into difficulty both planners and constructors. The idea to have a channel to collect part of the water represented a viable alternative. This was realized being actually a branch of the Danube, which crosses the neighborhood. This branch should now be reconverted, as it is a channel in which water does not circulate giving the image of a swamp with the afferent smell.

It is said that Petrzalka[267] was thought to be a city but built like a neighborhood. The big problem is the lack of public space, of landmarks, some direct-

Illustration 15: View over Petrzalka from the Bratislava Hrad. Image by the Author.

---

[266] On the website http://www.petrzalka.sk/en/buxus/generate_page.php?page_id=2027 accessed on 2nd september 2008, 15.45hrs.

[267] Prof. Ing. arch. Tibor Alexy, DrSc participant in the elaboration of the Petrzalka project held a speech at the beginning of the workshop telling a short unknown story.

ing axes and of a clear structure of the built space. We were to solve all these through proposed solutions during the workshop. We had to take into consideration the existing channel, which had to be reconstructed and given a new image and new uses. The area had to permit the construction of a new railway (of the TEN type), which should connect Vienna and Bratislava as well as other big cities in the area, belonging to a greater European project.

The chief architect of Bratislava[268] said that when problems at the outskirts appeared in Paris he was asked by a journalist if they shouldn't worry reminding of Petrzalka. His definite answer was NO, especially because in this neighborhood of Bratislava a pretty high percentage belongs to intellectual people unlike the situation of the outskirts of Paris, especially the Northern and North-Eastern part.

At the end of the presentation the organizers told us what they expected from us and which the problems of the identified area were. Here they mentioned the lack of public spaces and landmarks, the problem of social cohesion, the lack of directing axes, of interest poles as well as of force lines which should build connections with the rest of the city over the Danube.

ORGANIZING THE WORKSHOP.

In order to perform the theme the participants were divided into eight groups of each five students, each group being more or less coordinated by one or two tutors. I say more or less because some of the groups were supported by their tutors during the whole study, the others were only partly supported as some were missing for some days.

Having at hand four international and national architecture workshops I can suggest an opinion about the performance and organization way. Each of them was different because both of the identity difference of the cities and of the inhabitants and the geographic areas.

It is not recommended to start with the bad parts, but we have to take into consideration that this workshop had from the very beginning a major disadvantage: not presenting the details of the area to study, maybe because of the vast territory. Visiting the area would be like visiting a town like Medias, which is very difficult to do also because of the limited time for this work.

---

[268] Prof. PhD. Arh. Ing. Stefan Slachta, chief arhitect of Bratislava, in his opening speech of the workshop.

Thus, only a part of the neighborhood was presented, an area of the existing channel, and we had the occasion to observe Petrzalka from the height of the castle having a large perspective on the whole area and the neighbourhood.

The study began based on the short visit and the files on CD offered by the organizers representing satellite images (Google Earth), documents of .dwg format and some plans from the official town planning documentations.

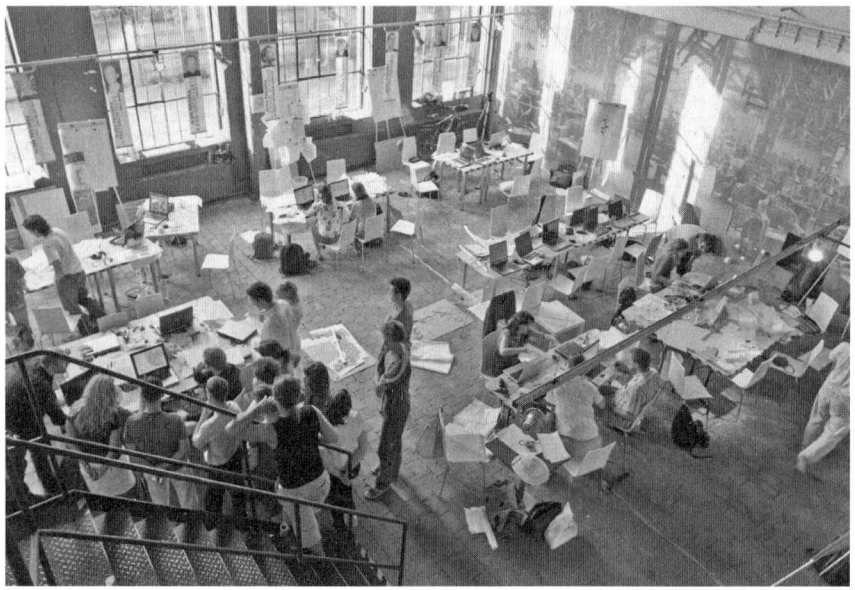

Illustration 16: Teams at work in the Design Factory. Image by the author.

The space for unfolding the work was a special one. The place was called Design Factory[269], a small art center created in an ex-furniture factory. Besides the offices of the personnel there were here a big room for presentations and conferences and an exhibition room where we had working tables, materials for models and panels for corrections and analysis. From this central room we had access to other two rooms, one for breakfast and lunch which was brought to us by catering and the other was called "chill-out room", where among the several pillows on the floor, the house shoos and the architecture magazines (in the Slovak language) there was a special equipped space for making lists during the study.

---

[269] The team DesignFactory is formed of three architects: Martin Paško, executive director; Zuzana Zacharová, commercial director; Zoran Michalčák, art director.

Illustration 17: The lecture and presentation of Thomas Ooms. Image by the author.

In the first three days we worked on defining the concept and analysing the existent situation and at the end of the third day there was the first and last correction on the organizers' part. The next two days were for finalizing and detailing the chosen concepts as well as for creating the models and final presentations. The sixth day was for writing down and sustaining the final projects. All these days were scattered with conferences and presentations of those present at the workshop. They represented architecture companies from Europe from the office in Vienna of Zaha Hadid[270] to small offices from the Czech Republic as A69[271] and Agents[272], but among them there were teachers from well-known institutions like the Experimental Study Department in Architecture of the University of Innsbruck and the University of SintLucas of Gent.

The result was different ways of approaching the concept of workshop and team work. While those from Zaha Hadid were combining the working hours with lectures and video-projections in order to stimulate and guide the parti-

---

[270] Team Zaha Hadid Studio Vienna: Robert Neumayr-Beelitz, Michael Budig, assistants of Zaha Hadid from Universities of Vienna and Innsbruck.
[271] The architect Jaroslav Wertig.
[272] Architects Štěpán Toman, Vendula Hladíková.

cipants, those from Agents preferred a different approach. Every one in the team was to work on a part of the project one day and the other day change the projects between them, and so on so that in the next five days everyone should bring his contribution to all project parts.

Besides those from Agents and Zaha Hadid there were other companies as Ynotarchitects, RDBM Architectens, Neutelings Riedijk, AI Design. I am sure that among these names the only one that you know is Zaha Hadid.

You come to know different people, you learn to work in a team, and you have the chance to break all barriers that society places. Besides this you can have contact with several situations and problems in the cities where the workshops take place and realize that the problems of town planning and architecture and the way these are solved are not very different form what happens in our country. Cultural differences and maybe the living standard of citizens are variables which can easily modify the existing situations.

Beside the hours of team-work most interesting were the presentations of the architects colleagues, who came as guides. I have to mention those of the colleagues from Zaha Hadid Studio, RDBM Architectens, Neutelings Riedijk, Agents. I would like to say a few words about them and with a bit of luck I will be able to bring them to Romania.

I was impressed by one thing in the presentation of the architect of Neutelings Riedijk[273], an architecture company from Rotterdam. He said they were thirty architects in the company divided into nine work teams, every team dealing with certain themes. He mentioned the fact that neither of them does the drawing part, all architects focus on the concept, and in the end they work with other offices or artists in order to finalize the front sides or the construction projects. I think this is the dream of any architect.

The colleague from RDBM Architectens of Belgium[274], who is also a teacher at SintLucas University in Gent, said at the beginning of the presentation that he did not like to talk about architecture so he would talk about books and music CD's and on the video-projector the book covers would appear together with images of the projects of the company he worked at. The message was extremely philosophic drawing the attention of everyone in the room. The way to present and his passion as if nobody was looking at him made this lecture be the only one, where nobody dozed; this happened not because of lack of respect but because we were very tired, as the conferences took place in the evening, after the working program.

---

[273] The young architect Joep van der Veen.
[274] The architect Tomas Ooms.

THE PROJECT OF STUDIO 6.

The Studio 6 team was formed of: Martin Bilek (the Czech Republic), Alexandru Calcatinge (Romania), Pavol Kasac (Slovakia), Dorota Mrazova (Slovakia), Katarina Valickova (Slovakia), and guides Stepan Toman and Vendula Hladikova (Agents, Czech Republic).

We called out project from the very beginning „Connections" because different connections had to be solved between the neighbourhood and the rest of Bratislava, among different areas of the neighbourhood and between the channel and the Danube. We tried the identification of several existing problems and their solving. Thus we worked upon five main areas: the connection area of the neighbourhood and the old center of the town, which had to be made across the Danube; analyzing and treating the whole channel of Petrzalka; the analysis of the relation built surroundings - natural surroundings; finding new centers in the neighbourhood and finding a guiding system in the neighbourhood.

The connection with the old town.
In the Northern part of the neighborhood there is the Danube, which at preset is not pointed out at the maximum, rather being a barrier between Petrzalka and Stare Mesto (the old town) than a bridge. We had to realize that bridge of the river, which was not at all easy. This area was analyzed in detail in the last part of the workshop. We proposed promenades on both sides of the river in order to benefit of its whole value, having as an example Paris and Budapest. We had also in mind new crossing walkways with artificial islands, which had to reduce the distance and offer functions for spending free time.

Analysis and treatment of the line crossed by the channel.
The neighbourhood Petrzalka is crossed by a channel of the Danube, which at present can not be navigated on and the water does not have a circuit while the connections with the river are blocked. Thus we proposed expanding the channel to permit navigation as well as rebuilding the river connections. We proposed a promenade with special corridors for bikers and pedestrians, with several areas for sports as well as areas with restaurants and terraces.

The relation between the built surroundings and the natural surroundings.

The neighbourhood had a lot of green area, which was not used at all, being left in its initial state; from satellite at least it seamed as a neighbourhood in full development. We proposed suspended terraces thus using the ground with commercial spaces, offices, so the superior level should have a public destination, terraces and suspended gardens. This thing was possible as there were initially built two levels, which were practically under ground, dwellings were only from the third level, which represented in fact the ground floor. In certain areas we could create all these spaces, without affecting the dwellings.

Finding new centers in Petrzalka.

It is pretty difficult to propose centers in an existing town or neighbourhood, as too many factors had to be taken into consideration. Theoretically, we could propose new centers in Petrzalka. First we analyzed the relation of the center of Bratislava with the whole city, thus observing that if we eliminate the neighbourhood Petrzalka, the center of the town is somewhere in the South-West, right on the bank of the Danube, next to Petrzalka. Thus we created the theory that by creating the center of Petrzalka on the right bank of the Danube, opposed to the historic center of the city, a new center is created, thus profiting by the advantage a river offers us by the four existing bridges. This is why the solution for the connectivity we followed seemed to be integrated and represent a coherent project. The study of the centers was maybe the most important having to be theoretically very well substantiated in order to sustain the solution. Starting from the definitions of the center and centralism, from the problems that cities' centers raise as well as from the theory of the central places of Christaller, we could find four new centers for Petrzalka, each of them with a different importance. Although the theory was applied at the level of geographic area, we applied it at the level of the city.

The space organization of a town reflects the culture, which led to its development and which can be traditional or modern. Any urban settlement has an adjoining area in which its influence is dominated. We used this at the level of the town taking into account the influence of certain dwelling complexes and areas of the neighbourhood. In order to determine the highest distance between two centers and their influence area we used a circle with its radius of 1.25 km, considering that this was a distance which can be walked in 5-10 minutes. This distance, compared to the highest length calculated between the Northern side of the neighbourhood and the Southern one, of 5 km, led to finding four centers, inclusively the one proposed on the bank of the Danube. We classified these as neighbourhood centers (two of them) and local centers (the other two), of complex[275].

Finding a guiding system in the neighbourhood. .

Petrzalka suffers because of the lack of identity, the monotony of the built space, which can easily lead to losing tourists or even inhabitants of another neighbourhood of Bratislava. Thus we had to come up with new ideas referring to the guiding way through the neighbourhood, which had to be both intuitive and confer the area a new identity. We based on different color systems at the level of dwelling complexes. A complex can differ from another by simply applying different colors at the ground floor of the buildings or at the level of the passers-by by using special signs. Another idea was to use where possible some signal buildings as perspective heads, different one from another, as some kind of a code, which tells you in what part of the neighbourhood you stand or in which dwelling complex.

Guiding was easier in open spaces, where there were large perspectives; the problem was inside different dwelling complexes, which in many places had the form of close polygons, where once being between the blocks you had the idea that you can no longer get out. We tried to analyze as many problems as possible and produce a well grounded concept with sketches, diagrams, schemes, photos with exemplifications and proposals for the neighbourhood Petrzalka.

---

[275] Classification by Lect. Drd. Arh. Gabriel Pascariu, in his lecture: „Zona centrala în marile orase", UAUIM, 2007.

Illustration 18: Scaled model of Studio 6 solution for Petrzalka. Image by the author.

IT IS POSSIBLE!

After taking part of such an event you ask yourself what you have learned, what you have accumulated after such an experience, how you broadened your knowledge horizon.

Conferences, if present, should be for most participants one of the most important events within a workshop. This is something that could be used in our country next to the work of the participants.

The purpose of the workshops is slightly different abroad than in our country. They look for concepts, well structured ideas based on a good theoretic part. They want possible solutions to the presented problems, without going too much into detail. „Brainstorming"[276] is most often used, thus obtaining the best from every team. In this case everybody has to forget about self-pride and have a single purpose, to have at the end a good result to a cer-

---

[276] In 1930 Alex Osborn elaborated a "group creativity" technique called **brainstorming**, created in order to increase the productivity of groups for solving problems. The basic idea must be known by everybody: Osborn said that by using these procedures groups could find more and better ideas than people working alone.

tain problem in a short period of time. It is about dedication, work under time pressure and maybe the wish to distinguish oneself.

The workshop has to be seen as a course for professional training, where participants assimilate or at least try to assimilate from the experiences of those who guide them. In our case each tutor presented the guiding lines which guided them in some successful projects.

Tomas Ooms presented books which were important to him and which guided him in the process of creation, such as „The silent takeover. Global capitalism and the death of democracy" by Noreena Hertz, „The Road" by Cormac McCarthy, „Sense of the City. An alternate approach of urbanism" Lars Muller Publishers, as well as music like Bach – The art of fugue.

The colleagues from Zaha Hadid Studio presented many projects made with students, town planning experiences using new concepts and theories as „flocking", „spiraling", „packing", using Voronoi diagrams, the L systems of the fracture theory as well as mathematic models taken from the growth of leaves.

This essay does not present only a description of a workshop, but it is an alarm signal that it is possible. It is true, in our country it is not possible (yet), but it is possible not far to the West. It is important both for the affirmation of Romanian architecture and for the architecture teaching to bring representatives of offices and teaching establishments to workshops with Romanian and foreign students.

Tomas Ooms was very receptive regarding a possible visit to Romania. He was personally fascinated about what the ex-Communist countries can offer, about the dedication and enthusiasm of young people and their wish to change something in their country. He was for the first time in Slovakia and he was pleasantly impressed by what he saw there. We have to go out of the shell built around us. We have to accept new visions, although they imply a certain risk of not being well received and understood.

I hope we will have the occasion to meet these architects and others too at workshops with local organization and enthusiastic students.

The Future of Symbolic Places

People objects – Studio 9

How can memory be an argument? We had the chance to experiment this in march 2007 in Mechelen, Belgium where we attended the International Architectural Workshop Dossin-Mechelen. The theme of the workshop investigated *The future of Symbolic Places*. The team I was in had seven members and the tutor was Caroline Sohie, senior architect at Arup Associates.

Our team's answer to the proposed theme was to use a series of pre existing data on the site in Mechelen, memories of the place, such as the wall (a witness to the atrocities of the Second World War – this being the place where the prisoners were executed) and the railway that was used to transport the remaining ones to the extermination camps in Poland and northern Belgium. Dossin was an old military barracks, used as a prison, a starting point from where jewish prisoners were deported to the camps.

The main element of the concept was the cell, a 3x3x3 modular cell, which was at the same time the icon of the collective and individual memory therewith. Thus we created, inside the old monastery building (vis-a-vis from the Dossin barracks), a matrix of cells, on three different levels, that was to become the Holocaust Museum. Walking through those cells opens to the visitor a series of spaces that tell a story about the atrocities of the Second World War in Mechelen and Belgium.

The cells represented the individual on his path, from the entrance in the Dossin Barracks to his transformation. Once in there, he would lose all his possessions and on his exist, he would only be a serial number, with no name, no identity, no past, no history, no personality. Thus, the cells go through the wall of the monastery, giving the impression of an escape. The path of the cells was straight to the wall and deeper in the ground, to symbolize the difficult path of the prisoner to his final destination, the death. Thus the path was deviated by the wall, a witness of history, and the cells will lose their cube shape, becoming prisms, more like coffins. In the end, their path ends at the entrance in the barracks.

Thus we tried to remake the individual's path from person to object, from life to death, from identity to number, through the path of the cells.

Bibliography

- Adorno, T. W., 2001. *Kant's Critique of Pure Reason*. Stanford, California: Stanford University Press.
- Adorno, T. W., 2007. *Minima Moralia*. Bucuresti: Editura ART.
- Arendt, H., 2007. *Condiția Umana*. Cluj Napoca: Editura Ideea Design.
- Aristotle, 1959. *Politics*. Cambridge: Harvard University Press.
- Aristotle, 2008. *Physics*. Oxford: Oxford University Press.
- Aristotle, 2008. Politics, Book III, Chapter 3. *In*: Meagher, S. M., ed. *Philosophy and the City*. Albany: State University of New York Press, 33-39.
- Ballantyne, A., 2002. *Architecture. A very short introduction*. Oxford: Oxford University Press.
- Ballantyne, A., 2004. *Architectures. Modernism and after.* Oxford: Blackwell Publishers, 2004.
- Ballantyne, A., 2007. *Deleuze and Guattari for Architects*. London: Routledge.
- Banham, R., 1960. *Theory and Design in the first Machine Age*. London: Architectural Press.
- Bartetzky, A., Schalenberg, M., 2009. Shapes of Happiness. *In*: Bartetzky, A., Schalenberg, M., ed. *Urban Planning and the Pursuit of Happiness*. Berlin: Jovis Verlag GmbH, 7-17.
- Bell, D., 1978. *The Cultural Contradictions of Capitalism,* New York: Basic Books Inc. Publishers.
- Benjamin, W., 1999. *The Arcades Project*, London: The Belknap Press of Harvard University Press.
- Benjamin, W., 2007. *Illuminations*, New York: Schocken Books.
- Bennett, T., 2001. *Differing diversities. Cultural policy and cultural diversity.* Strasbourg: Council of Europe Publishing.
- Bird, G., 2006. *The revolutionary Kant: a commentary on the Critique of pure reason*. Chicago: Open Court Publishing Company.

- Black, I. S., 2003. (Re)reading architectural landscapes. *In:* Robertson, I., ed., *Studying cultural landscapes.* London: Arnold, 19-46.
- Bridge, G., Watson, S., 2000. City Imaginaries. *In:* Bridge, G. and Watson, S., ed. *A Companion to the City.* Oxford: Blackwell Publishers Ltd, 7-18.
- Buttimer, A., 1993. *Geography and the Human Spirit.* Baltimore: The Johns Hopkins University Press.
- Carrier, J., 2003. Mind, Gaze and Engagement: Understanding the Environment, *Journal of Material Culture*, Volume 8 (5), pp. 5-23.
- Clark, T., 2002. *Martin Heidegger.*London: Routledge.
- Compagnon, A., 1998. *Cele cinci paradoxuri ale modernitatii.* Cluj-Napoca:Editura Echinocțiu.
- Cook, I. et. al., 2005. Positionality/Situated Knowledge. *In:* Atkinson, D., et. al., *Cultural Geography. A critical dictionary of key concepts.* London: I B Tauris & Co Ltd.
- Cosgrove, D., 2008. *Geography and Vision. Seeing, Imagining and Representing the World.* London: I.B. Tauris & Co Ltd.
- Coverley, M., 2010. *Psychogeography*, Herts: Pocket Essentials.
- Crang, M., 2003. Cultural Regions and their uses: the interpretation of landscape and identity. *In: 1st Conaculta Conference on Regional Cultures*, 2003, Quereterao, Mexico.
- Crary, J., 2002. Spectacle, attention, counter-memory. *In:* McDonough, T., 2002. *Guy Debord and the Situationist International: texts and documents.* Cambridge: MIT Press.
- D'Angelo, M., 2000. *Cultural policies in Europe: local issues.* Strasbourg: Council of Europe Publishing.
- Davis, T., 2010. Third Spaces or Heterotopias?, *Sociology*, volume 44 (4), pp. 661-677.
- Debord, G., 2002. *The Society of the Spectacle.* Canberra: Hobgoblin Press.
- Dewey, J., 2008. Philosophy and civilization. *In*: Meagher, S. M., ed. *Philosophy and the City.* Albany: State University of New York Press, 110-114.
- Edwards, J., 2009. *Language and Identity.* Cambridge: Cambridge University Press.
- Encyclopaedia Britannica 2008 Ultimate Reference Suite, Chicago, 2008

- Foti, M. V., 2003. *Vision's invisibles. Philosophical explorations.* Albany: State University of New York Press.
- Foucault, M., 1996. *Cuvintele si lucrurile,* Bucuresti: Editura Univers.
- Foucault, M., 2001. Alftfel de spații. *In:* Foucault, M., *Theatrum Philosophicum.* Cluj-Napoca: Casa Cărții de stiința.
- Frampton, K., 2007. *Modern Architecture. A Critical History.* London: Thames & Hudson.
- Frisby, D., 2007. *Cityscapes of Modernity.* Cambridge: Polity Press.
- Gelven, M., 1989. *A commentary on Heidegger's Being and Time.* Rev. ed. Illinois: Northern Illinois University Press.
- Georgiu, G., 1997. *Națiune,cultura,identitate*, Bucuresti: Editura Diogene.
- Giedion, S., 2002. *Space, Time and Architecture. The growth of a New Tradition.* 5th ed., 14th printing. Cambridge: Harvard University Press.
- Giraldi, L., 2005. Cultural Planning: an integrated approach to regeneration. *In: INHERIT Symposium*, 2005 Goteborg.
- Glassie, H., 2000. *Vernacular Architecture.* Bloomington: Indiana University Press.
- Gordon, E., et. al., 2008. Placeworlds: Using Virtual Worlds to Foster Civic Engagement, *Space and Culture*, volume 11, pp. 204-221.
- Harrison, R., 2009. Excavating Second Life: Cyber-Archaeologies, Heritage and Virtual Communities, *Journal of Material Culture*, Volume 14, pp. 75-106.
- Heidegger, M., 1971. Building Dwelling Thinking. *In:* Heidegger, M. *Poetry, Language, Thought.* London: Harper & Row, 143-161
- Heidegger, M., 1977. The Age of the World Picture. *In:* Lovitt, W., ed. *The Question Concerning Technology and Other Essays.* New York: Harper Torchbooks, 115-154.
- Heidegger, M., 2003. *On the Way to Language.* New South Wales: HarperCollins Publishers Ltd.
- Heidegger, M.,2006. *Problemele fundamentale ale fenomenologiei.* Bucuresti: Humanitas.
- Heynen, H., 1999. *Architecture and modernity: a critique.* Cambridge: MIT Press.

- Hirsch, E., 1995. *Anthropology of Landscape.* Oxford: Clarendon Press.
- Hollander, J., et. al., 2009. Commentary: Virtual Planning: Second Life and the Online Studio, *Journal of Planning Education and Research*, pp. 108-113.
- Hubbard, P., 2006. *City. Key ideas in geography.* New York: Routledge.
- Inglis, D., 2010. Civilizations or Globalization(s)?: Intellectual Rapprochements and Historical World-Visions, *European Journal of Social Theory*, Volume 13, No. 1, pp. 135-152.
- Inwood, M., 1999. *A Heidegger Dictionary.* Oxford: Blackwell Publishers.
- Ioan, A., 2002. Arhitectura interbelica si chestiunea identitatii colective, *Caietele Echinox* 3/2002, Fundatia Culturala Echinox, pp. 80-91.
- Jackson, J. B., 1984. *Discovering the Vernacular Landscape.* New Haven and London: Yale University Press.
- Jackson, J. B., 1994. *A Sense of Place, a Sense of Time.* New Haven and London: Yale University Press.
- Jaguaribe, B., 2005. The Shock of the Real: Realist Aesthetics in the Media and the Urban Experience, *Space and Culture,* Volume 8, pp.66-82.
- Jameson, F., 1998. *The Cultural Turn. Selected writings on the Postmodern.* London: Verso.
- Johson, P., 2006. Unravelling Foucault's 'different spaces', *History of the Human Sciences*, Volume 9 (4), pp. 75-90.
- Jordan, P., 2009. Place names as ingredients of space-related identity. In: Jordan, P., et. al. Eds. *Geographical Names as a Part of the Cultural Heritage.* Vienna: Institut fur Geographie und Regionalforschung, 33-39.
- Kant, I., 2000. *Critique of Pure Reason.* Cambridge: Cambridge University Press.
- Kant, I., 2004. *Prolegomena to Any Future Metaphysics that will be able to come forward as Science.* Cambridge: Cambridge University Press.
- Kaplan, F., 2009. *1959: The year that everything changed.* New Jersey:Wiley and Sons Inc.
- Kunzmann, K., R., 2004. Culture, creativity and spatial planning.

The Town Planning Review, 75 (4), Liverpool University Press, pp. 383-404.
- Löwy, M., 2009. *Morning star: surrealism, marxism, anarchism, situationism, utopia*. Austin: University of Texas Press.
- Lyotard, J-F., 2003. *Conditia postmoderna*, Cluj-Napoca: Editura Idea.
- Maciocco, G., 2008. *Urban Landscape Perspectives*. Springer.
- Matei, A., 2004. *Identitate culturala locala*, Cluj-Napoca: Editura U.T. PRESS.
- McDonough, T., 2002. Situationist Space. *In:* McDonough, T., 2002. *Guy Debord and the Situationist International: texts and documents*. Cambridge: MIT Press.
- Mekking, A., 2009. The Architectural Representation of Reality: The Built Environment as the Materialization of a Mental Construct. *In*: Mekking, A. and Roose E. ed. *The Global Built Environment as a Representation of Realities*. Pallas Publications, 23-51.
- Mercer, C., 2006. Cultural Planning for urban development and creative cities. Paper for Shanghai Cultural Planning Conference, 2006.
- Merleau-Ponty, M., 2009. *Phenomenology of Perception*. New York: Routledge.
- Mihali, C., Copoeru, I., 2002. *Cartografii ale modernitații*. Cluj-Napoca: Editura Casa Carții de stiința.
- Mitchell, D., 2000. *Cultural geography. A critical introduction*. Oxford: Blackwell.
- Mumford, L., 2008. Retrospect and Prospect. *In*: Meagher, S. M., ed. *Philosophy and the City*. Albany: State University of New York Press, 125-133.
- Murdoch, J., 2006. *Post-structuralist geography. A guide to relational space*. London: Sage Publications.
- Nieuwenhuys, C., 1959. A different City for a different Life. *In:*McDonough, T., 2002. *Guy Debord and the Situationist International: texts and documents*. Cambridge: MIT Press.
- Palermo, P. C., 2008. Thinking over Urban Landscapes. Interpretations and Courses of Action. *In:* Maciocco, G. ed. *Urban Landscapes Perspective*. Springer, 27-43.
- Pallasmaa, J., 2005. *The Eyes of the Skin. Architecture and the Senses*. West Sussex: John Wiley & Sons Ltd.

- Park, R. E., 1926. The Concept of Position in Sociology. *In: Publications of the American Sociological Society*, Vol. 20, 1-14.
- Plato, 2008. *Timaeus and Critias.* Oxford: Oxford University Press.
- Robins, K., 2006. *The Challenge of Transcultural Diversities.* Strasbourg: Council of Europe Publishing.
- Robson, M., Stockwell, P., 2005. *Language in Theory. A resource book for students.* Oxon: Routledge.
- Ross, K., 2002. Lefebvre on the Situationists: an interview. *In:* McDonough, T., 2002. *Guy Debord and the Situationist International: texts and documents.* Cambridge: MIT Press.
- Sadler, S., 1999. *The Situationist City.* Cambridge: MIT Press.
- Sauer, C. O., 1963. The Morphology of Landscape. *In:* Leighly, J., ed. *Land and Life. A Selection from the Writings of Carl Ortwin Sauer.* Berkley: University of California Press, 315-350.
- Self, W., 2007. *Psychogeography.* London: Bloomsbury.
- Sharr, A., 2009. *Heidegger for Architects*. London: Routledge.
- Simmel, G., 2008. The Metropolis and Mental Life. *In*: Meagher, S. M., ed. *Philosophy and the City*. Albany: State University of New York Press, 96-101.
- Simon, B., 2006. Beyond Cyberspatial flâneurie. On the Analythic Potential of Living with Digital Games, *Games and Culture*, volume 1 (1), pp. 62-67.
- Stanculescu, F., 1935. Stil romanesc si stil modern. *Revista Arhitectura, 1/1935,* pp. 13-14.
- Stout, F., 2000. Visions of a New Reality: The City and the Emergence of Modern Visual Culture. *In*: Le Gates, R. T., et. al. ed. *The City Reader.* 2nd ed. New York: Routledge, 143-149.
- Swarts, D., 1997. *Culture and Power. The sociology of Pierre Bourdieu.* Chicago: University of Chicago Press.
- Tanase, Al., 1968. *Introducere în filosofia culturii.* Bucuresti: Editura stiinţifica.
- Taylor, T., L., 1999. Life in Virtual Worlds: Plural Existence, Multimodalities, and other Online Research Challenges. *American Behavioral Scientist*, 43 (3), Sage Publishing, pp. 436-449.
- Trask, R. L., 2010. *Language. The basics.* Oxon: Routledge.
- Tuan, Y., 2008. *Space and Place. The Perspective of Experience.* Minneapolis: University of Minnesota Press.

- Vaneigem, R., 1961. Comments against Urbanism. *In:* McDonough, T., 2002. *Guy Debord and the Situationist International: texts and documents.* Cambridge: MIT Press.
- Vianu, T., 1982. *Studii de filosofia culturii.* Bucuresti: Editura Eminescu.
- Vidler, A., 2008. *Histories of the Immediate Present. Inventing Architectural Modernism.* Cambridge: MIT Press.
- Wearing, S., et. al., 2010. *Tourist Cultures: Identity, Place and the Traveller.* London: Sage Publications Ltd.
- Weber, M., 2008. Concepts and Cathegories of the City. *In*: Meagher, S. M., ed. *Philosophy and the City.* Albany: State University of New York Press, 102-109.
- Werner, J., 2004. *American flâneur: the cosmic physiognomy of Edgar Allan Poe.* New York: Routledge.
- West-Pavlov, R., 2009. *Space in Theory.Kristeva, Foucault, Deleuze.* New York: Rodopi.
- Whyte, I. D., 2002. *Landscape and History since 1500.* London: Reaktion Books Ltd.
- Williams, J., 2005. *Understanding Poststructuralism,* Bucks: Acumen Publishing Limited.
- Wilson, C., 2003. *Everyday America. Cultural Landscape Studies after J.B. Jackson.* Los Angeles: University of California Press.
- Zukin, S., 2000. Whose City? Whose Culture?. *In*: Le Gates, R. T., et. al. ed. *The City Reader.* 2nd ed. New York: Routledge, 131-143.

Illustration Index

Illustration 1: Jackson's vision on space. Graphic by the author...65
Illustration 2: Yi-Fu Tuan's vision on modern urban space and awareness. Graphic by the author..67
Illustration 3: Graffiti drawing in Vienna. Territorial marker as a face. A metaphorical view on landscape as face. Image by the author...69
Illustration 4: Language as a component of cultural landscape. Peter Jordan's vision on language and place names. Graphic by the author..70
Illustration 5: Sketch on the idea of visions. A layer structure of the cultural landscape as a palimpsest. Graphic by the author..71
Illustration 6: Image by the author of an Oil Painting courtesy of Amelia Prostean. Reproduction with prior consent of the artist..72
Illustration 7: The view of a house through a water-soap baloon. A metaphor of seeing the city: is not just an image, is a representation that needs to be interpreted, decoded and understood. Is a complex of symbols and signs that lets you see only a snapshot of the real (e.g. in the photo the house) but in the same time warns you about the multitude of interpretations (e.g. in the photo there are two different views of the same house in only one baloon, from one point of observation – the photographer's position). Image by the author......................77
Illustration 8: The Palace of Parliament, former People's House, in Bucharest, Romania, the second largest building in the World after the U.S. Pentagon. Image by the author...............79
Illustration 9: The author's vision on cultural landscape, it's components and the connections between the existing cities that create a continuous dynamic change. Graphic by the author. 81
Illustration 10: The "Scanteii" House, built between 1952 and 1957 in Bucharest. It's destination was to accommodate the State's Publishing services. After 1989 it's name changed into "The House of the Free Press". It's architecture was inspired by Russian Leningrad Hotel and Lomonosov University buildings and is similar to the Palace of Culture in Warsaw, Poland. It was a symbol of power. The power of the written word in the Socialist regime. Image by the author...85
Illustration 11: View over downtown Bucharest by night. Image by the author......................113
Illustration 12: View over the Tarnava Mare river valley from the high hills of Medias, in central Romania. In the background are the Fagaras Mountains. Image by the author................115
Illustration 13: View over the small town of Medias and the Tarnava Mare river valley. Image by the author..115
Illustration 14: The eight Development Regions of Romania. Map designed by the author.....116
Illustration 15: View over Petrzalka from the Bratislava Hrad. Image by the Author..............130
Illustration 16: Teams at work in the Design Factory. Image by the author..............................132
Illustration 17: The lecture and presentation of Thomas Ooms. Image by the author..............133
Illustration 18: Scaled model of Studio 6 solution for Petrzalka. Image by the author.............138

Alphabetical Index

A

a posteriori	60
a priori knowledge	25, 28, 60
a priori representation	25
a way of imagination	15
Aart Mekking	73
Adam Sharr	30p.
André Breton	86, 91
Antoni Gaudi	43, 47
Aristotle	19pp.
Art Nouveau	45

B

Bart Simon	109
Bauhaus	42, 44, 47, 49, 98

C

Carl Ortwin Sauer	50, 54, 60, 76
Charles Baudelaire	86p.
CIAM	96
Claude Levi-Strauss	56
CoBrA	98pp.
Colin Rowe	45p.
counter-space of the metropolis	52
creative process	14p.
cultural concept	57, 74
cultural isolation	37
cultural planning	13, 113, 115, 124, 126pp.
cultural symbol	51, 83
cyberspace	104, 108p.

D

Dasein	27
David Frisby	73, 89
David Serlin	94
dependency on spatial perception of time	32
Design Factory	132
dialectic of the social space	111
distinctive character of the concept	106
Don Mitchell	54
duality of reality	27
Duiliu Marcu	48

E

Edgar Allan Poe	88
empiric concept	26
environmental determinism	54p., 60p.
Eric Gordon	106, 108
Eric Hirsch	78

F

Frank Lloyd Wright	43

G

Georg Simmel	74, 95
Graham Bird	24
Guy Debord	86p., 98p., 102

H

Hannah Arendt	74
Heidegger	16pp., 27pp., 36, 57
Helen Keller	94

Henry Glassie	55	lyric functionalism	81
heterotopia	84, 106	**M**	
Hilde Heynen	50		
hybrid cultural space	18	manifestation of language	38
		manifestation of the politics	50
I		Marcel Iancu	48
Iain S. Black	75	mathematic spaces of the urbanism	
ideality of space	27	and modern architecture	97
identity of a community	36	Max Weber	74
Imaginist Bauhaus	98	media production symbols	16
inter-relation of space	52	mental construct	15, 72p., 113
inter-subjective value	39	mental images	15p.
International Journal of Arts and Sciences	13	Merlin Coverley	86p.
		metaphoric way	73
Ion Mincu	7, 48	methaphysical and transcendental expositions	24
Ivan Chtcheglov	96		
		Michel Foucault	40, 59, 111
J		milieu	74
J.F Lyotard	36	modern cosmopolitan flâneur	108
James Carrier	109	MUVE	107
James Werner	88	**N**	
Joel Henry	93p.		
John Brinckerhoff Jackson	62, 97	New Babylon	100
John Leighly	76	new globalization era	51
Jonathan Crary	103	**O**	
Jonathan Murdoch	56		
Justin Hollander	107	Octav Doicescu	48
K		**P**	
Kant	19, 23pp., 57, 60	Paul Klee	44
		Petrzalka	135
L		Peter Jordan	7, 69
Laszlo Moholy-Nagy	44	Petrzalka	135
Le Corbusier	44, 46p., 64, 80, 98	Petrzalka	129pp., 136p.
Lefebvre	75, 78, 99p., 106, 111	Phil Hubbard	111
Lettrist Group	86, 97	Philosophic influences	55
Lewis Mumford	75	Pier Carlo Palermo	78
Lonely Planet	93p.	place names	69pp.
Louis Henri Sullivan	44	Plato	19p.

plural space	15	system of relations	75, 77, 113
power of integration	38	**T**	
power relations	40		
proximity	15, 53, 118	tactile space	15
psychogeography	86p., 96, 98p., 112	Teresa Davis	106
R		the cultural moment	18, 57, 59
		the sense of vision	15
Raoul Vaneigem	101	the stroller	88pp.
reading and decoding the landscape	53	Theodor Adorno	79
		Tim Ingold	110
relation object - text	73	Tom McDonough	102
reversibility	20p.	transcendental aesthetic	25
Romania	139	Trevor Barnes	111
Robert Ezra Park	82	Tudor Vianu	54p.
Roland Barthes	111	types of locomotion	22
Romania	80, 87, 116, 134p., 139	**U**	
Russell West-Pavlov	78		
S		urban image	76, 85
		V	
schizophrenic	68, 105		
second life	105	Veronique Foti	16p.
Second Life	107p., 112	vicinity	41, 73
sense of place	64pp.	Victor Horta	43, 47
sense of the world	68	virtual world	106p., 109p., 112
sensitivity of space	15, 75	visual space	15
Sharon Zukin	74, 82	**W**	
Sigfried Giedion	45		
situational knowledge	59	Walter Benjamin	86, 88pp., 95
Situationist International	98p.	Walter Gropius	44, 64
social implications	83	Wassily Kandinsky	44
society of spectacle	18, 105	Will Self	87
spaces and symbols of life	52	William Morris	43
spiritual identity	39	**Y**	
symbolic meaning of the landscape	52	Yi-Fu Tuan	66, 107

ABOUT THE AUTHOR

Alexandru Calcatinge was born in the town of Medias, in Romania, in February 1983. He is a young architect, member of Romanian Architect's Order (O.A.R.), a freelance photographer and a postgraduate student in architecture and urban studies. He has a master degree in regional development and territorial planning from the University of Architecture and Urban Planning „Ion Mincu" in Bucharest, Romania, and he currently is a PhD candidate in urban studies at the same university. His major research topics are on cultural landscapes, cultural planning and regional development, with a major interest in urban cultural landscapes.

He had a scholarship for his PhD research in Austria, at the University of Vienna, Department of Geography and Regional Research in 2009/2010, under the supervision of HR Prof. h. c. Univ.-Doz. Dr. Peter Jordan from the Austrian Academy of Sciences and is a member of ECOVAST Austria and ISUF (U.K.) and one of the founders of the cultural association TAM-TAM (Young Artists of Medias) in Romania.

Alexandru Calcatinge is a Open Source and Free Software advocate. This book was created by using only free software like Ubuntu Linux operating system, OpenOffice.org, Inkscape for graphics and Gimp for photo processing. Thus he strongly recommends using free software as it is a matter of freedom.

More informations about him you can find on:
www.calcatinge.ro and www.visionsofthereal.com